More Cornish Murders

John Van der Kiste
& Nicola Sly

The History Press

First published 2010
Reprinted 2012

The History Press
The Mill, Brimscombe Port
Stroud, Gloucestershire, GL5 2QG
www.thehistorypress.co.uk

British Library Cataloguing in Publication Data.
A catalogue record for this book is available from the British Library.

ISBN 978 0 7524 5545 7

Typesetting and origination by The History Press
Printed in Great Britain

CONTENTS

INTRODUCTION & ACKNOWLEDGEMENTS

The chance to write *More Cornish Murders* came as a welcome opportunity for both of us. Firstly, we were able to cover some of the fascinating historical murders that lack of space forced us to omit from our first jointly-written book, *Cornish Murders*, published by The History Press in 2007. Since then, we have both independently written several books. Compiling this further collection of true cases gave us the chance to work together again, something that we both thoroughly enjoyed.

Like *Cornish Murders*, our second compilation covers murders the length and breadth of Cornwall, some of which attracted national publicity, others which were practically unheard of beyond the county borders. The featured cases include murders committed in the course of robberies, such as the 1811 murder of Isaiah Valentine in Fowey and the murder of Roger Drew in St Stephen-by-Launceston in 1862. Some murders are the work of jealous lovers, such as the one perpetrated in Pool in 1952 by Bertha Mary Scorse. Others, like the 1958 'Green Shirt' murder in Newquay and the killing of schoolgirl Edith Mary Parkin near Nanstallon in 1922, remain unsolved to this day. Details of the cases were drawn mainly from contemporary local and national newspaper reports, which are listed in more detail in the bibliography.

As always, there are numerous people to thank for their assistance. The staff from The Cornish Studies Library in Redruth proved a great help in collating the research material. On a more personal note, Richard Sly and Kim Van der Kiste helped immensely with proof reading and also took some of the photographs used as illustrations.

Finally, as always, we must thank our editors at The History Press, Matilda Richards, Beth Amphlett and Jenny Briancourt, for their continued help and encouragement.

Every effort has been made to clear copyright, however our apologies to anyone we might have inadvertently missed; we can assure you it was not deliberate but an oversight on our part.

John Van der Kiste & Nicola Sly, 2010

ALSO BY JOHN VAN DER KISTE

ALSO BY NICOLA SLY

1

'FOR GOD'S SAKE LET ME GO'

Fowey, 1811

Isaiah Falk Valentine was a German Jew who came to England, probably in the early years of the nineteenth century, as a reader or preacher to the synagogue in Plymouth. While he was there he became a friend of William Wyatt, landlord of the Jolly Bacchus in Plymouth Dock, which later became Devonport. Unfortunately, their association was destined to end in a less-than-friendly fashion.

Later, Valentine decided to make a living by travelling around the country selling jewellery and purchasing guineas. It was in this capacity that on 16 November 1811 he received two letters from Wyatt, who had recently moved to Fowey, where he was running the Rose and Crown. The latter invited him to come and meet him, saying that he had some pieces to dispose of, and that he wanted to introduce him to another gentleman who could also offer him some items for sale.

Valentine came to Fowey three days later. When he arrived at the Rose and Crown, Wyatt behaved oddly, prevaricating at first. For almost a week he kept putting Valentine off with one excuse after another. At length, on 25 November, he suggested they should go for a walk together, and he took Valentine to the Broad Slip in Fowey, saying that they had an appointment to meet a Captain Best. This was nothing less than a ruse to lure him to the waterside. When they arrived, the more strongly-built Wyatt overpowered his trusting companion, grabbed hold of him, seized £260 in notes from his pockets, and threw him over the edge.

As he walked through the churchyard back to the inn, his boots squelching loudly, two boys asked what he had been doing, but he ignored them. At the Rose and Crown he carefully concealed the money, £260 in notes, in a dung heap behind the building, on the assumption that this was the safest place to leave it. When he went back into the bar, only about twenty minutes after having left, a man who had seen him and Valentine going out together asked him what had happened to the other man.

'Have you not heard that he was drowned?' Wyatt answered. 'I tried to save him, but could not.'

Shortly afterwards a couple of men brought the body of Valentine to the inn, and it was laid in an outhouse until the authorities could be informed and a post-mortem held. As landlord and itinerant trader had been noticed in each other's company, it was inevitable that suspicion would fall on the survivor. When enquiries were made, there were several witnesses ready to testify that Valentine had gone out with Wyatt, and the latter was immediately taken into custody. After a post-mortem, Valentine's body was interred in the Jewish burial ground at Plymouth.

Two days later a thorough search of the premises was made inside and out, and the missing money was found in the dung heap. The notes were identified as having been Valentine's property by the Hebrew characters on the back of each.

At the inquest, Wyatt defended himself by explaining that while they were on the beach, Valentine had gone into the privy, and after coming out he fell into the water. He himself made every effort to rescue the poor man, but in vain. Nevertheless, the jury did not accept his defence, and a verdict of wilful murder was returned against him.

Wyatt was brought to trial at Launceston Assizes on 26 March under Sir A. Chambre. Two witnesses who had been at the scene of the killing said they had

Fowey Harbour. (Authors' collection)

heard a man exclaim repeatedly in a foreign accent, 'Oh, Mr Wyatt, for God's sake let me go.' Wyatt continued to plead 'Not Guilty', and showed nothing but indifference throughout the eleven-hour hearing. As the evidence was largely circumstantial, he was probably confident that he would walk away from the court a free man.

The press reported that when the jury announced their verdict of 'Guilty', and the judge sentenced him to death, he became very 'agitated'. Nevertheless he behaved like a model prisoner during the next few weeks, and freely confessed to the chaplain and authorities that he had indeed been guilty of the crime.

On 30 April, Bodmin was packed with visitors who had come to watch his execution the following day, and that night there was barely a spare bed to be had. As dawn broke the next morning, every street around the gaol was crowded. At about 10 a.m. Wyatt appeared on the platform, and contrary to the usual practice, did not address the spectators.

His execution did not go according to plan. After the hangman had placed the noose around his neck and was about to let the drop fall, Wyatt fell, the rope slipped on his neck, and the knot nearly came under his chin, leaving the windpipe free from pressure. The noise he made trying to breathe during his death agony was heard by those closest to him, and it was about twenty minutes before he died. After being cut down, it was reported that 'his body was given to his friends who are all respectable persons.'

2

'AN IRISHMAN AND A CATHOLIC'

George Stevenson worked as a servant to the Price family at Kenegie near Penzance. Late in the evening of 12 December 1813, while riding home, he saw a body lying in a field, and stopped to investigate. The victim was wearing a sailor's uniform, and there was a trail of blood leading from the gateway of the field to the body.

On arriving at Kenegie, he informed Mr Price, who went to look at the body with him. They reported it to the authorities, and the dead man was identified as John Allen. Enquiries revealed that on 9 December Allen had been seen in a public house with William Burns, a recruit belonging to a party of artillery, now stationed at Penzance. Allen had been staying in the town until late on the night of Saturday 12 December, when he left to return to his station.

Burns was found at Penzance and arrested on suspicion of murder. When apprehended, he was ordered to turn out his pockets and threw down a 9in-long brown net purse, with a tassel on one end and two yellow slides, containing 19s. As the constable searched him thoroughly, a blue and white handkerchief was found between his shirt and his skin. Although he insisted that the purse had been given to him by his uncle, witnesses came forward to say that both items had belonged to Allen. He realised there was no point in contradicting them or giving any further explanation as to how it had come into his possession.

At an inquest at Penzance, Burns was charged with wilful murder and committed to Bodmin Gaol. He did not deny being an accessory to the murder, but insisted he was not solely to blame. There were several others, he said, who were equally if not more responsible for the deed than he was, and he intended to incriminate them.

When he went on trial on 29 March 1814, there were several witnesses for the prosecution. One was the landlady of the Seven Stars, Penzance, where Burns and Allen had been billeted. On the morning of 9 December, she had tied some biscuits up in a blue-and-white spotted handkerchief for Allen's lunch. Four days later, she saw Burns when he came in unusually late, and she asked him why he had not slept in his bed on the previous night. He told her that he had arrived back at about 11 p.m. and found the house locked, so he slept in the stable. Unfortunately for him, she was able to tell him – and the court – that she had not gone to bed herself until after midnight, and if he had arrived back an hour earlier he would have seen the light on in the house.

Above: *Land's End.* (*Authors' collection*)

Left: *Kenegie, now a hotel and country club.* (*Authors' collection*)

Another witness, Lieutenant Ratsey, commander of the signal station near Land's End, had known Allen well and could corroborate the evidence regarding his possessions. He confirmed that the purse and the handkerchief, both produced in court, had been Allen's property.

After all the evidence had been heard, Burns was asked whether he had anything to say in his defence. He told the court that he was an Irishman, and had not been in England for long. As a complete stranger to the area, who had known nobody in Penzance for more than a few days, he was being made a scapegoat for the crime

The Seven Stars public house in Penzance. (© N. Sly)

of another person. If only he had had the chance to get to know people better, he might have been able to call into court some of those who had seen him in the street at the time he was said to have been with Allen. As it was, he had no witnesses to call, and he was throwing himself entirely on the merciful consideration of the court and the jury.

It was to no avail, and the jury found him guilty. In summing up, the judge told him that he had been convicted of the highest crime known to the law, on evidence which left no possible room for doubt. When he observed that Burns was about to reply, he told him sternly not to add falsehood to the load of guilt which already rested on him, and urged him to use the short time he had left to live in seeking mercy at the hand of his offended Creator. On hearing the verdict, Burns seemed quite unmoved and walked firmly from the court to his cell without betraying any emotion on his face.

There had been much general revulsion in the area at his crime, and it was reported that some of the witnesses had come from Penzance to the courtroom not only to give evidence but also to watch him being condemned to death, after which they would return home in triumph. The horses and the driver of the chaise in which they left were dressed in ribbons, 'as symbols of the exultation which they felt on the occasion'. The *West Briton* commented in disgust at such a callous display of inhuman joy at his fate, however well-deserved it might have been. Their glee, it said, 'would disgrace savages; it was diabolical, even though he was an *Irishman* and a *Catholic.*'

On the evening of 30 March, one of the prison officers wrote to the editor of the same paper that the condemned man had confessed to his guilt, had constantly prayed to God for forgiveness since being committed to gaol, and was deeply pained for having denied the fact in court. 'He is very penitent and I think will continue so to the last.' He went to the gallows on the following day.

3

'I'LL SHOOT YOU FIRST'

During the Anglo-American conflict of 1812-5, several contingents were sent from the West Country to fight in the United States. In August 1814 one such company of soldiers from the 28th Foot Regiment, quartered at Pendennis Castle, was under orders to proceed by forced marches to Plymouth and then embark for their voyage across the Atlantic.

As their baggage passed through Lostwithiel on 21 August, four members of the guard who had been drinking at an inn in the town remained behind when the party moved forward, oblivious to the fact that their comrades had gone on and left them behind. Two of them, John Sims and Richard Rogers, were so drunk that the other two could not go on without them. Shortly after midday they asked Constable William Hicks if he could help them to requisition a cart which would take them on to the next town. Hicks and a magistrate, who was passing by at the time, firmly told them that it was not their job to help, and the men had no automatic right to expect additional transport. When he asked them who would meet the expense if it was provided, they brusquely replied that it was the duty of the government. Hicks told them that as soldiers they ought to know better than that. Sims denied that he was drunk, and insisted that he would not be seen riding on a cart, presumably because he considered it beneath his dignity as a soldier. Realising that they were getting nowhere, they walked away, and Hicks, hoping he had seen the last of them, closed the door.

Ten minutes later they were back. Sims had evidently had second thoughts, and they asked if somebody could take them in a cart to Liskeard. Hicks said that if they were prepared to pay, he would arrange it for them. They enquired how much it would cost, and Hicks told them it would be 12s. Sims asked Rogers to pay, and Hicks stipulated that the money would have to be paid before he went to any effort to help. 'I'll be damned if I do, I'll walk,' muttered Rogers, as he left.

When the soldiers left Hicks's house a second time, Rogers went to see another man who he hoped would pay part of the money. Sims sat on some steps before Miss Sparnon's house, a few doors away on the same side of the street. While sitting there, James Netherton, who lived opposite Hicks and had been sitting at his window while the conversation took place, heard Sims say that he would have the blood of some person before he left the town. He had already muttered something about shooting Hicks, who had retreated quickly into his house and shut the door.

Angry at being thwarted, as they walked down Fore Street they fixed their bayonets, threatened some people standing by, and muttered that they would fire through the constable's door as they charged their muskets with the ball cartridges handed out to them as part of the luggage guard. One of them, probably Rogers, presented his musket in different directions, making half-hearted attempts to fire randomly at various people standing in the street. Luckily for them he had not loaded it properly, and it failed to go off. Even so, the alarmed crowds begged him to be careful, but he took no notice.

Immediately afterwards Sims stopped, fixed his bayonet, and stood as if ready to fire. Rogers called out to him to load his musket, as he was sure that the 'Cornish buggers' were going to murder him. At this time there were some boys and youths standing near the house, but they were keeping quiet and certainly knew better than to say or do anything that might seem provocative to these soldiers.

Lostwithiel. (Authors' collection)

As they continued down the street, they were met by Joseph Burnett, an officer of the peace responsible for maintaining law and order in the town. He told them firmly that any man trying to cause a public disturbance would be taken into custody at once.

'I'll shoot you first,' Sims retorted. He rested his musket on the wheel of a cart in the street in front of Burnett, and warned him that if he advanced an inch he would not hesitate to fire.

Rogers tried to unfasten his pouch, but he was so drunk that Sims had to help him. He took out a parcel of cartridges, one of which he gave to Rogers, who managed to prime and load his gun with assistance. After the bayonet was fixed Rogers walked unsteadily a few yards down the street, where he pointed at a group of people and tried to fire. When the piece flashed in the pan, Sims said angrily that the gun was good for nothing, and he would load his own. As they continued down the street together, Burnett came out of his front door to follow both men. Rogers turned round, pointed his weapon at him, and the piece again flashed in the pan. Undaunted, Burnett followed them round the corner, and a shot was fired.

Burnett moved to one side, as Sims raised his musket, stepped back a few paces, levelled at him and fired. The ball entered Burnett's breast, passing through his body and striking Walter Davies, a bystander who was immediately behind him, shattering his backbone. Both men fell to the ground, mortally wounded, as spectators seized both soldiers and their weapons. Had Rogers' musket still been loaded, and had they not acted promptly, he would probably have fired and killed somebody else as well. Sims tried to keep crowds at bay with his bayonet for a while, until the combined effort of several men managed to hold him securely and wrest the weapon from his grasp.

Burnett was carried into a nearby house. James Netherton, a friend who lived nearby and had seen what was going on, stayed by his side, but there was nothing that could be done for him. He breathed his last about half an hour later.

Davies lingered for another three days, and died on 24 August. Both had left large families, Burnett being the father of nine children and Davies of five. An inquest into Burnett's death was held on 22 August, and a verdict of wilful murder was returned against John Sims and Richard Rogers for the murder of Burnett, though not of Davies.

They appeared at Bodmin Assizes in March 1815, and several witnesses from Lostwithiel were called by the prosecution to give their recollections of the fateful day. Constable Hicks recounted the conversation he had had with the prisoners regarding their demands for transport to Liskeard, and he said that Sims appeared sober and Rogers drunk at the time. James Netherton, who had observed events at close quarters and seen the smoke coming from Sims's gun immediately after the fatal shooting, corroborated this evidence.

Several other witnesses were examined in court. They unanimously agreed that, in view of the prisoners' disorderly conduct in wantonly brandishing their muskets with fixed bayonets in the street, and threatening to shoot people for no reason whatsoever, Burnett had done no more than his duty in coming forward to prevent

The chapel, Bodmin Gaol. (Authors' collection)

any injury from being inflicted on innocent bystanders. He had been warned that their muskets were loaded, and while he might have been unwise in assuming they would not fire at him, he did not flinch from his responsibility as he asked them to follow him into the nearest inn and surrender their arms.

In their defence, the prisoners claimed that they had been threatened by the townspeople and were only protecting themselves from possible mob violence. This carried no weight with the jury who found Sims guilty. But, to general astonishment, they acquitted Rogers. Sir Robert Graham immediately pronounced sentence of death on the former. An order was issued for his execution on the subsequent Friday, and for his body to be sent for dissection after being cut down.

Sims had been in the army for twelve years and he took the verdict without any visible sign of emotion. During his last few days in custody, he admitted to the chaplain at Bodmin Gaol that habitual drunkenness was to blame for his bad behaviour. It was an occupational hazard for many soldiers at the time. The Devil found work for idle hands to do, and so often the demon alcohol was simultaneously the bored soldier's best friend and worst enemy. His mother saw him three times after he had been sentenced to death, and he asked her to write to his brothers, also in the army, begging them not to fall into his bad ways, and to heed his sorry fate as a warning. After conducting himself 'with becoming resignation and fortitude', he went to the gallows shortly after midday on 31 March 1815.

4

'IF YOU DON'T COME OUT I'LL BUTCHER YOU'

Boscastle, 1821

On 7 April 1821 a party at Boscastle was celebrating the wedding of Joseph Paul and his bride. As was to be expected, the company gathered for the occasion had a great deal to drink after the ceremony. Among the guests present were Nicholas Gard, Henry Hoskin and Joseph Bray, each of whom spent much of the day going from one public house to another and drinking several pints of beer at every one.

At one stage, Paul handed Hoskin 2s to buy some snuff which they could all share after the wedding. Some of the hardened drinkers in the gathering suggested that the money would be better spent on beer than snuff. Gard and Hoskin had never really liked each other, and during what became an increasingly heated exchange, Gard called Hoskin a bastard, at which Hoskin slapped him in the face and walked away.

Vowing to seek revenge, Gard threatened to fight him. Without issuing a formal challenge to settle the issue with his fists or any other way, he walked the few yards to his house, and fetched one of the knives which he used in his trade as a shoemaker. Taking care to conceal the weapon, he then rejoined the assembled company, who were standing in the street at the time.

Choosing his moment carefully, he rushed at Hoskin and stabbed him in the stomach. The knife went in between two of the ribs and pierced the heart, and Hoskin collapsed on the ground, bleeding from the chest, nose and mouth, dying almost at once. A crowd of women screamed, and the alarm was raised. Meanwhile Gard ran away and he tried to seek shelter in several houses in turn, but was refused admittance. Eventually he concealed himself in a hedge in a nearby garden. Richard

Above & below: *Boscastle. (Authors' collection)*

Benoke, who lived in the street and had come out of his house to see what the noise was about, went in search of him and found him later that afternoon.

William Pearce, a local surgeon, was called to conduct the post-mortem examination on Hoskin's body. He found that the cause of death was a large cut, about an inch long, on the right-hand side of the right breast. On opening the body, he found that the wound had penetrated to the chest. Gard's knife had perforated the coronary artery.

After being held in custody at Bodmin Gaol on a charge of murder, he went on trial on 23 August. As there had been such a large number in the wedding party, there were plenty of witnesses for the prosecution. Everyone summoned was ready to testify to the ill-feeling between prisoner and deceased. All of them agreed that the argument had started over a dispute as to how the 2s given to them by Paul should be spent, although their recollections of what went on immediately before the fatal blow varied slightly.

Joseph Bray recalled Hoskin taking off his smock frock as if in readiness to fight, saying that he had owed Gard a grudge, and would repay him. Jane Hocken said she had seen Gard return to his own house after the quarrel had erupted, and go indoors, but come out again almost immediately afterwards, calling him rude names and saying, 'I am ready for thee,' to which Hoskin answered, 'If thou art a man come out.' Gard, she continued, said he was not prepared to come any further than the door. When Hoskin advanced to strike him, Gard held up his right hand to ward off the blow, struck Hoskin with the left, and then heard a loud shriek from Betsey Prout, another of the women present.

A couple of witnesses were called by the defence. The first was Abel Greenwood, who had known both deceased and prisoner, and had been in the inn when the argument started. He said that as far as he was aware, both men were previously on good terms. However, Hoskin was taller, stouter and younger than Gard, 'and was given to passion like other men'. Not more than ten minutes had elapsed from the time Hoskin hit Gard, until Hoskin collapsed and died. It was regrettable, he ventured, but hardly surprising, that matters should have ended in this way.

He was followed by Gard's wife Ann. She told the court that she had been in the house when the dispute occurred, and her door was not shut. Hoskin had come in through the front door, saying, 'I will pay thee.' He then stripped to his shirt, and threatened her husband, 'If you don't come out I'll butcher you,' at which she asked him to leave. This must have been at the time that her husband returned to fetch the knife, but she had no recollection of seeing the weapon at any stage, or indeed noticing if Hoskin had anything in his hand at the time. Fearing for their safety, and alarmed that somebody might try and set the house on fire, she asked her husband to go out for a while.

Their evidence did nothing to sway the members of the jury. After the judge's summing up, they were only out for ten minutes before they found Gard guilty of murder. While in court he had given every impression of confidence in being discharged, but when sentence was passed and he was led back to gaol, he seemed stunned.

On the morning of 10 September he knelt for a short time in prayer with the prison chaplain, told him that he put his trust in Jesus, and died in charity with all men. He expressed contrition for what he had done, forgave his enemies, and proclaimed he was not afraid to die. Later that morning he was led to the gallows.

5

'DEAR DEVIL, KEEP AWAY FROM ME THAT I MAY REST ALONE'

Calenick, near Truro, 1830

Sixty-five-year-old William Andrew worked in the smelting works at Calenick and lived with his wife, Grace, in a terraced cottage in the village. By all accounts, their marriage had been a long and happy one, producing two children who were now grown-up and had moved away from home, a son to Plymouth and a daughter to Truro.

On 20 January 1830, William went to bed at his normal time of between eight and nine o'clock. Usually, Grace would accompany William into the bedroom and the couple would say their prayers together. Then Grace would kiss her husband goodnight and go back downstairs to catch up with the household chores, before joining William in bed when she had finished. William was profoundly deaf in one ear and was in the habit of sleeping on his side, with his 'good ear' pressed to the pillow – in that way, he was guaranteed a good night's sleep, undisturbed by any noise that Grace or his neighbours might make.

Unusually, William woke up at about two o'clock on the morning of 21 January, to find that Grace had not yet come to bed. He got up and went to the top of the stairs, calling her name, but the cottage remained ominously quiet, so William went downstairs to see where she was.

The cottage had very few rooms – a bedroom upstairs and a sitting room and kitchen downstairs, from which a door opened into the communal passage shared by other occupants of the block of terraced cottages. When William got downstairs, he immediately noticed that the door leading out into the passage was open, even though it had been closed when he went to bed.

The cottage was in complete darkness and William had no light with which to search for his wife. He knocked on the doors of the adjoining houses, until he managed to rouse the families who lived there. John Bray and John May accompanied him back to his house with lamps and found the body of Grace Andrew lying face-down in her sitting room, the back of her head smashed like an eggshell, apparently by blows from a blunt instrument. A small table knife was clutched in her hand, with which she had evidently tried to defend herself against her attacker.

The police were summoned and found themselves faced with a mystery. There was no trace of any possible murder weapon at the Andrews' home and the house showed no signs of any struggle having taken place. Grace Andrew's clothes were undisturbed and, at first glance, nothing seemed to be missing from the premises.

William Andrew told the police that his wife was in charge of the couple's finances and that all their savings were kept in a locked chest in their bedroom, the key to which Grace always carried in her pocket. When the police searched Mrs Andrew's clothing, the key was indeed found in a pocket in the bosom of her dress but, when it was used to open the chest, over £50 in Bank of England notes and gold sovereigns were missing. It seemed as though whoever had attacked and killed Grace Andrew had first taken and then later replaced her key, rifling through the box in the bedroom in the meantime, all without disturbing her soundly-sleeping husband. When questioned, two of Mrs Andrew's neighbours said that they had heard noises coming from the house at around half-past nine in the evening. Eliza Bate heard what she believed to be Grace Andrew laughing out loud, followed by five or six loud blows. Eliza thought nothing of what she had heard, since Grace Andrew was known to chop sticks and break coal for the fire on the floor and, to Eliza, it sounded as though she was doing just that. Grace Bennett, with whom Eliza was spending the night, lived next door to the dead woman and heard exactly the same thing, although she described the noise made by Grace Andrew as a brief cry rather than a laugh. Grace Bennett agreed with Eliza, saying that the sounds seemed nothing out-of-the-ordinary.

An inquest was opened into Grace's death by coroner Mr J.H. James. As always, the coroner's jury were required to inspect the body and, on this occasion, they were also expected to search the chest where, according to William Andrew, his life savings should have been. The newspaper reports of the time record that the chest was 'minutely examined' but no trace of the missing cash was found and the coroner theorised that perhaps Grace Andrew had taken to carrying it about her person without her husband's knowledge. It was strongly believed that the murderer was someone who was familiar with the Andrews' home and routines but, by the conclusion of the inquest, the police had found absolutely no clues to enable them to identify Grace Andrew's killer and the coroner's jury therefore returned a verdict of 'wilful murder against some person or persons unknown'.

Grace Andrew's burial was planned for Monday 25 January and, that morning, William suddenly recalled the funeral of a relative some years earlier. On that occasion,

Calenick. (© N. Sly)

he had worn a pair of black gloves and he decided that they would be appropriate for his wife's interment service. William remembered that the gloves had been stored in the same locked box from which his savings had been stolen and, as he was searching though the contents of the box for his gloves, he came across a small parcel containing the missing money. Thirteen individual sovereigns had been carefully sewn between two pieces of silk cloth and a pocket stitched to the silk held the bank notes.

Since the inquest into Grace Andrew's death had already concluded, after this new development the case was taken up by magistrate Mr Humphrey Willyams. Every single item had previously been removed from the chest in the search for the missing money and there was no dispute that, at the time, the money wasn't there. The fact that it appeared to have been replaced in the four days since the murder strengthened the belief that Grace Andrew's killer was someone who was not only familiar with the household but who also had access to the house after the murder. Thus, Willyams focused his enquiries on the Andrews' near neighbours, all of whom had been in and out of the house, caring for William.

The block of terraced houses was occupied by several families and, in addition, there was a small dwelling at the back of the terrace, where Mrs Jane Ninis lived with her daughter Elizabeth Bate and granddaughter Eliza. Elizabeth had heard William Andrew trying to rouse John Bray and John May prior to the discovery of the body and had rushed to see if she could help. Since the murder, numerous people had visited William Andrew, including his daughter Mrs James and her friend Mrs Williams, Jane Ninis, Elizabeth and Eliza Bate, Grace Bennett and all the members of the Bray and May families. None of the visitors could remember anyone having unsupervised access to the box in the bedroom – with two exceptions.

On the Sunday after the murder, Mrs James and Mrs Williams were with William Andrew when Jane Ninis came to visit. Mrs Ninis was not a particularly pleasant old lady and Mrs James soon tired of her presence, suggesting to her friend that they went into another room. However, Mrs Ninis was quite unable to take a hint and immediately followed them. Eventually, all three women went upstairs with William Andrew, who wanted to get a clean shirt out of the box.

When he had done so, his daughter and her friend left the room to give him the privacy to change but Mrs Ninis stayed put in the bedroom, so that William was forced to move out onto the landing to remove his soiled shirt and put on his clean one. When interviewed, Mrs Ninis had a different recollection of what had happened, saying that she too had gone downstairs with Mrs James and Mrs Williams. Yet both of those ladies and William clearly remembered that she had remained in the bedroom alone with the unlocked box while William changed his clothes.

The only other person who had access to the box was Mrs Ninis's granddaughter, Eliza Bate. Eliza had been very close to Grace Andrew and, on the morning of the funeral, had helped William to look for his gloves in the box. William was understandably quite agitated at the time and Eliza had been a little distressed to see him 'tumbling about' his late wife's clothes as he searched. She knelt on the floor and helped him sort more carefully through the garments stored in the box and was thus present when the money was found. Obviously, William was within touching distance of her throughout the search for the missing gloves and was later to insist that she could not possibly have put anything into the box without him noticing.

At the conclusion of the inquest into Grace Andrew's death, coroner Mr James had an account of the proceedings transcribed and sent a copy to the then Home Secretary, Mr Peel, with a request for assistance in solving the mysterious murder. Peel responded by sending a Bow Street Runner, Mr Ellis, to help the local magistrates with their enquiries, as well as authorising a reward of £100 for information leading to the conviction of the culprit or culprits.

The murder was now under investigation by three local magistrates, as Mr W. Peter and Revd R. Polwhele joined forces with Mr Willyams. Still believing that the murder had been committed by someone who knew the victim well, the magistrates re-interviewed William Andrew and his neighbours. William was apparently deemed to be above suspicion but John and James Bray and John May were arrested. They were kept in custody for three days and subjected to intense questioning by the magistrates, who found not a shred of evidence against any one of them, and eventually all three were released without charge.

The enquiries continued without further progress until March 1830, when two brothers named Skewes came forward with information about Peter Matthews, a lodger in their home. Matthews had originally been arrested and interrogated by Mr Ellis, the Bow Street Runner, but had been released due to lack of evidence. With the announcement of the reward for information, the Skewes brothers tried again to implicate Matthews in the murder of Mrs Andrew.

The three investigating magistrates held a private meeting in the Council Hall at Truro, during which they took sworn statements from all the principal witnesses in the case and, the following day, a public meeting was held. There, the depositions of the witnesses were read out and Matthews was consequently charged with the murder and committed for trial at the next Assizes. Protesting his innocence, he was taken to prison to await the start of the proceedings against him.

Matthews was due to appear at the Lent Assizes. However, having considered the prosecution's case, the Grand Jury determined that there was insufficient evidence against him to warrant a trial by jury. A decision of 'No bill' was returned and since Matthews hadn't been specifically named as the murderer at the inquest, and so could not be tried on a coroner's warrant, there was no option but to discharge him.

It was another two years before the alleged killer of Grace Andrew appeared before Mr Justice Park at the Assizes in Launceston and, once again, the defendant was thirty-year-old Peter Matthews, who still pleaded 'Not Guilty' to the charge against him.

When the proceedings opened on 28 March 1832, prosecution counsels Mr Tancred and Mr Follett outlined the events of the 20 January 1830 for the court before calling their first witness, William Andrew.

Andrew was followed into the witness box by John Bray junior and John May, who related finding the body of Grace Andrew. Both men knew the defendant and both had seen him in the vicinity of the Andrews' home two days before the murder, when he had actually visited John Bray senior. Elizabeth and Eliza Bate and Grace

Truro, c. 1960. (Authors' collection)

Bennett also gave evidence. All had known the defendant for between fifteen and twenty years and believed him to be a man of good character.

Matthews was a native of Calenick, who worked as a stone mason and, prior to the murder, spent some time living and working in Mexico. On his return to England in 1829, he took up lodgings with Catherine and Henry Skewes in Fairmantle Street in Truro, sharing a room and a bed with one of their two sons, James.

In the weeks prior to the murder of Grace Andrew, the Skewes family testified that Matthews had been very short of money and one night shortly before the murder, James heard him say, 'I must have money. I will be damned, but I must have money.'

When James asked him where he intended to get this money from, Matthews outlined a plan to break into the home of Mr and Mrs Andrew by smashing a window pane at the back of the house, unlatching the window and climbing through it into the house. 'I know he has money or spoons or something,' Matthews told James.

When James said that Mr and Mrs Andrew would hear him breaking the glass, Matthews told him, 'To be sure they will. I'll carry my lath hammer with me and soon do their business for them.'

James Skewes was himself short of money and Matthews tried to persuade him to join him in robbing Mr Andrew. 'Do you mean it?' James asked him, not quite able to believe that he was serious. Matthews assured James that he did and, a week before the murder, he told James that he had been to the Andrews' house and seen the couple sitting by the fire. 'I trembled like a rush,' said Matthews.

On the night of the murder, James Skewes met with a friend, Thomas Atkinson, and was consequently a little later than normal retiring to bed. Peter Matthews got into bed with him at about half-past ten and, unusually, was up early the next morning, claiming that he couldn't sleep.

As James lay awake in bed, he heard Peter talking to his father downstairs, saying 'There was a pretty job done at Calenick' and informing Henry Skewes that Grace Andrew had been hit over the head with a 'flat polled instrument' and killed. By the time James had dressed and gone downstairs, Matthews had left but James later met him on Tabernacle Street in Truro and questioned him about the fate of Grace Andrew.

Fairmantle Street, Truro. (© N. Sly)

'Peter, is that your job at Calenick last night?' James asked him and, when Peter assured him that it wasn't, James pointed to some red stains on Peter's waistcoat and asked him what they were. Peter swore that the red spots were not blood and continued to insist that he had nothing whatsoever to do with the murder. He told James that he was mistaken about the time at which he had come to bed the night before, saying that it was closer to half-past nine than half-past ten. As the days passed, James continued to pump Peter for information on the murder but Peter persisted in denying all knowledge of it. 'If I had done it, wouldn't I have money?' he asked James, who pointed out that he had most probably hidden it.

In court, Catherine Skewes corroborated James's recall of the time at which her lodger had returned home and gone to bed on the night of the murder and she also testified to washing a waistcoat for him that appeared to be spotted with blood.

Cross-examined by Mr Crowther, the counsel for the defence, James maintained that he had said nothing to anyone about the lodger's plans before the murder because he truly believed that Matthews was just joking. Once Mrs Andrew had been killed, James insisted that he feared for his own life but had continued to sleep with the lodger to try and 'sift the fact out of him'. He had spoken to his brother, Thomas, on the day after the murder and discovered that Matthews had also tried to persuade Thomas to join him in robbing the Andrews. However, although both brothers had been interviewed by Bow Street Runner, Mr Ellis, they chose to wait until the reward of £100 was offered before revealing the majority of their allegations against Matthews.

Various aspects of the Skewes brothers' accounts were verified by other witnesses. Their sister, Mary Gilbert, confirmed that Matthews had frequently spoken of robbing someone and 'knocking their brains out' to get some money. Mary too had thought he was joking and, like her brothers, had not taken Matthews's remarks at all seriously until after the offer of the reward was publicised. Thomas Atkinson agreed that he had spent the evening of the murder with James, who had left him to go home at around twenty-five minutes past nine.

A man named Lambert Pidwell told the court that, on 20 January, he had been playing cards with Matthews in a beer house until about half-past eight, when Matthews left. John May had also been there and he too remembered Matthews leaving the beer house at that time, adding that it was located just over a mile from Calenick village.

Matthews seemed to have discussed the murder with several other people. Nicholas Kent, a labourer from Calenick Street in Truro, recalled talking to him and saying that he believed the police suspected William of killing his wife. 'It is not the old man. I can clear him,' said Matthews. Another man, Thomas Pidwell, remarked that the presence of the knife in Grace's hand was a curious thing. 'She took it off the table,' explained Matthews, as if he had been in the room at the time and seen her doing so.

A lath hammer was produced in court, along with several witnesses who swore that it belonged to Peter Matthews. Among the witnesses was Thomas Skewes, who said that on the night of the murder, he had seen Matthews walking towards Calenick with the hammer sticking out of his pocket. Surgeon James Ferris of Truro had conducted the post-mortem examination on Grace Andrew, finding five wounds on her head with corresponding skull fractures and brain damage. Ferris described one wound as 'incised', one as 'semicircular' and the remaining three as 'small punctures'.

Having examined the lath hammer, Ferris was of the opinion that the two different ends of its head could have produced all of Mrs Andrew's injuries. Ferris had removed Mrs Andrew's scalp during the post-mortem and was able to compare the size and shape of her wounds with the head of the defendant's hammer. A second doctor, Clement Carlyon MD, concurred with his colleague's conclusions. Having seen the dead woman's scalp, he later tested a dozen different types of hammer and, after comparing the shapes of their heads to the victim's injuries, concluded that a lath hammer, such as the one owned by Matthews, was the most likely murder weapon.

In 1831, Peter Matthews went away to sea, serving on board the ship *Dublin*, which sailed to Rio de Janeiro. The prosecution called William Hallett, a private in the Royal Marines, who served aboard the same ship.

Both Matthews and Hallett had been ill while on board and had slept in adjacent hammocks in hospital. Night after night, Matthews had kept Hallett awake tossing and turning and talking loudly in his sleep, apparently addressing the Devil.

'Dear Devil, keep away from me that I may rest alone,' shouted Matthews.

According to Hallett, in his more lucid moments, Matthews had told him that he had killed a woman near Truro with a stone hammer. He mentioned that the woman's husband was deaf and that, although he had expected to obtain a lot of money from robbing the couple, he had actually got very little.

Hallett reported the conversation to the doctors attending the two men and Matthews was confined in the ship's hold as a prisoner. He was arrested on his return to England and charged with the murder.

Most of the witnesses who had given evidence for the prosecution testified that Matthews came from a respectable family and was of good character, including William Andrew, who told the court that he and Grace had known Matthews since he was a young boy and had never had any quarrel with him. Andrew added that he had not seen the defendant near his house prior to the murder and neither had Matthews visited him afterwards, so he would have had no opportunity to return the money had he stolen it, having first murdered Mrs Andrew.

Although Mr Crowther called no witnesses for the defence and Peter Matthews declined to speak when offered the opportunity to testify, his original statements to the magistrates, taken on 13 March 1830, were read out in court. At that time, Matthews accused the Skewes family of having a grudge against him and insisted that he knew nothing about the murder and had not been in Calenick for a fortnight or more when Mrs Andrew was killed. Matthews's statement remained unchanged at his second appearance before magistrates on 26 December 1831, when he continued to deny all knowledge of the murder.

Once Mr Justice Park had summed up the evidence for the jury they retired only briefly before pronouncing Peter Matthews 'Not Guilty' of the wilful murder of Grace Andrew. Matthews was discharged from the court a free man.

Although the contemporary newspaper accounts of the murder lack sufficient detail to draw any firm conclusions, it seems evident on reading them that the one person who could most easily have returned the missing money to the locked box after the murder was William Andrew himself. If the reported witness statements are to be believed, only Jane Ninis and Eliza Bate had the opportunity to tamper with the box after the inquest, and the thought of such an old lady or her young granddaughter being responsible for the brutal killing of Grace Andrew, and subsequently returning the stolen money, seems incredible. It seems equally fanciful to contemplate that, if robbery was indeed the motive for Mrs Andrew's murder, her killer would return the money to the chest. Anyone concerned at having the missing money in his or her possession could just have easily discarded it, hidden it or even dropped it somewhere in the Andrews' house – why would the killer take the risk of replacing it, even assuming that he or she could gain access to the key?

The killer or killers of sixty-three-year-old Grace Andrew were never brought to justice and, so long after her untimely death, her murder is destined to remain a mystery that will never be solved.

Note: The Bray family is described in the contemporary newspapers as comprising John Bray, his wife, two grown-up sons and a fifteen-year-old daughter, all of whom resided in a cottage in the same terrace as Mr and Mrs Andrew, most probably next door. The May family is described in less detail, the only member specifically mentioned being John May, although Jane Ninis was John May's mother-in-law. When members of the two families were arrested on suspicion of having murdered Grace Andrew, it is not clear whether John and James Bray are father and son or the two grown-up sons of John Bray senior.

6

'WHY DID YOU NOT LEAVE YOUR FATHER?'

Looe, 1834

Twenty-nine-year-old John Henwood worked as a butcher at Looe. He lived with and helped his seventy-two-year-old father, also John, and his mother Anne, at Treloy, their farm in the parish of St Martins, near Looe. Father and son had never really been on the best of terms, and years of simmering discontent came to a head on the morning of 7 August 1834.

Shortly after breakfast, the father told his son to go to the field with three of the labourers and mix some lime. A little later the father went on horseback to the field, found his son doing nothing, and scolded him mildly for not doing as he had been asked. The latter argued that he was carrying out his instructions as requested. His father then told him to go and mix the lime, and both men walked towards a pile of the substance. The son, now in a thoroughly bad temper, took a shovel and pick and started throwing lime around at random.

'If you don't do as I bid you, you shall leave,' his father told him sharply. The son retorted angrily that he had no intention of doing his work any other way, and called his father 'an old, thick-headed fool'. He threw his tools down on the ground, adding that his father was like an old bear, and 'all his sorrows were to come'.

The elder man then rode off, and the son left the field not long afterwards. His mother was surprised to see him back at the house so soon, and asked him whether the lime was not fit for use. He said it was not, and he had come back to spin some straw ropes instead. Going upstairs, he unlocked a box in which he kept a supply of gunpowder and, taking with him the key of the cider cellar, walked into the orchard and continued through the fields beyond. Mrs Henwood also came out of the house, perhaps having a presentiment that something was not quite right.

A little while later, several other workers in the area heard a gunshot. One of them, Thomas Pengelly, had seen John Henwood the younger leaving the field where he had been working, and he heard Mrs Henwood cry out in horror that her husband was dead.

Pengelly, who suspected what must have happened, and the three Henwood daughters went to see for themselves. There had been some rain that morning, and the ground was wet. A tell-tale line of footprints, in which the right foot was turned out at an angle, was clearly visible. John Henwood the younger, who had trouble with his foot, was known to have a rather peculiar walk. Pengelly followed this line through the orchard hedge, across several fields and to a gate bordering on a lane. Here he found the body of John Henwood the elder, lying on his face. He called some of the other labourers, and when they picked up the body, a bullet wound near the heart was visible. They felt for a pulse, but he was obviously dead.

The rest of that day was spent searching for John Henwood the younger, but there was no sign of him, and he did not return home. On the following afternoon William Rickard and Mr Hender, labourers who worked for Mr Jory, a neighbouring farmer, found him looking over a hedge.

'Oh, John, I am sorry to hear of the accident that has happened to your father,' Rickard said, 'and I am told you are the man that caused it.'

John admitted he was responsible. 'Rickard, you have children,' he continued, 'mind keep them at a distance, and don't give them their way; it has been my ruin; he is gone, and I shall not be long behind.'

'Why did you not leave your father, if you could not live with him?' Rickard asked.

'You little know what I have gone through, these six months or more,' was the reply. Rickard and Hender gently began to lead Henwood away, but Henwood shook them off, assuring them he could go by himself. He made no effort to escape as they walked with him, and when they reached Mr Jory's farm he willingly gave himself up. During the previous twenty-four hours or so, the news had rapidly spread by word of mouth.

Richard Chiswell, a miller who lived at Morval, was passing by. 'Oh, John, what have you done,' he said, 'I am told you have murdered your father.' Henwood nodded, admitting it was 'a bad job'. When Chiswell added, 'I should have thought that when you saw your father coming your heart would have failed you.'

'Yes, it did at first,' Henwood answered. 'I put the gun to my shoulder, and then took it down again. Something then told me I must do it, and I put it up again, and it was off in an instant.' When they asked him where the gun was, he told them he had left it in a hedge at the bottom of a nearby field. One of them went to find it, and brought it back, and Henwood confirmed it was the gun he had killed his father with, as he had no other.

The Summer Assizes at Cornwall had finished that same day, so John Henwood had to endure seven months in custody. He went on trial at Bodmin Assizes on

28 March 1835 for the wilful murder of his father before Mr Justice Pattison, with Messrs Smirke and Tyrrell for the prosecution. His mother Ann was one of those to give evidence about what happened that fatal day, the others being Rickard, Hender and Chiswell. Fourteen-year-old John Harris, who lived with the Henwoods, also spoke about the events leading up to the elder man's death. Henry Box, a surgeon from Looe, said that the bullet had penetrated the left breast of the deceased, breaking four of the ribs and penetrating the heart and lungs.

In the younger Henwood's defence, James Oliver, a farmer from Morval, said he had known him for about thirteen years. Everyone, he recalled, considered the man rather stupid, and he had seen boys and girls making 'game of him', calling him 'foolish John Henwood'. One of his sisters was an idiot. He did not think the young man was dangerous, and the fact that he had carried on a successful trade as a butcher for six or seven years suggested he was not completely hopeless, even if he might be somewhat simple-minded. Richard Bray, who had been to school with him, said he regarded Henwood as a pleasant young man but he lacked commonsense, and everyone treated him as a fool. Peter Toy, a carpenter who lived near Treloy and who had known Henwood all his life, told the court that some time ago after an argument with his mother about a pudding, he had threatened to hang himself, and fetched a rope for the purpose. Only Toy's powers of persuasion had saved him from such a disastrous course of action. Charles Pearse, Henwood's brother-in-law, spoke of how he had seen him in the field one day threatening to shoot himself, and again he would have done so had Pearse not prevented him. Further witnesses who had known Henwood for some time corroborated these assertions, pointing out that he had always been considered 'of weak intellect'.

The condemned cell, Bodmin Gaol. (Authors' collection)

None of this was sufficient to establish a case for suggesting that the patricidal young man was not responsible for his actions when he committed the fatal deed. After all the evidence had been heard the judge summed up, telling the jury that there could be no doubt the prisoner had killed his father. Their verdict would depend on whether he was capable of knowing right from wrong, and how aware he was of the consequences of what he was doing. He may have been born foolish, but that did not necessarily make him insane.

The jury retired for a little over an hour. While they were out, Henwood looked less concerned than anybody else in court. When they returned, he gazed at them with some anxiety, and when the foreman delivered their verdict of 'Guilty', his face fell, and there was a marked alteration in his appearance. He was sentenced to be executed on the following Monday, and his body would be buried in the precincts of the gaol. As he was removed from the bar, he muttered, 'Lord have mercy on me!'

While he was in Bodmin Gaol waiting for the sentence to be carried out, the chaplain had several conversations with him. It emerged that before the trial took place, Henwood had somehow convinced himself that he could not be convicted, as nobody had seen him fire the fatal shot. He confessed his guilt, and expressed repentance for having killed his father. He said he had been very upset not long before the killing, as a young woman he had been fond of was angry with him for flirting with other girls, and he had decided to kill himself. It was in this frame of mind, he said, that he took out his frustrations and anger on his father instead.

In accordance with the judge's instructions, he went to the gallows shortly before midday on 30 March.

7

'SOMEONE HAS GOT IN AND KILLED POOR MRS SEAMAN'

Penzance, 1845

It was a red-letter day in the town of Penzance, as the foundation stones for both the new pier and the new market place were being laid. Thus, on 7 July 1845, the whole town was in a carnival mood. There was a procession, after which most of the residents crowded around to watch the ceremonies.

The inhabitants of Rosevean Road went to join in the celebrations, with the possible sole exception of Mrs Elizabeth Ruth Seaman, who was apparently busy packing for a house move. Forty-seven-year-old Mrs Seaman was the widow of a solicitor from Swansea, who died aged seventy-six in 1842, leaving her both property and money. A well-educated and good-looking woman, she shared her house with sixty-one-year-old Benjamin Ellison, a man she called 'cousin', although many believed that they lived together as man and wife. Ellison, from Halifax in Yorkshire, was a former lieutenant in the militia and, whatever his relationship with Mrs Seaman, the couple had both made wills, each leaving all their worldly goods to the other.

At midday, a volley of shots rang out over Penzance as the laying of the foundation stones was heralded with a gun salute. At that time, a woman passing by Mrs Seaman's house heard what she described as 'fearful, dreadful, horrid groans' coming from within. She was too frightened to stop and investigate further but the source of the moaning noise became evident the very next morning.

Benjamin Ellison was seen entering his house at half-past eight and, half an hour later he appeared at the door of his next-door neighbour, Mrs Hill. He politely asked

Above & below: *Penzance, 1950s. (Authors' collection)*

Rosevean Road, Penzance. (© N. Sly)

if she would mind coming to his house and, as they were crossing the back yard together, he told her, 'I slept out last night. Someone has got in and killed poor Mrs Seaman.'

'Good God. Is it possible?' exclaimed Mrs Hill, and tearfully Ellison assured her that it was.

Mrs Hill bravely went into the house and found Elizabeth Seaman lying dead in the front room. The floor was awash with blood and there were splashes and smears all over the walls. Mrs Seaman appeared to have been laid out. She was wearing her day clothes, which had been neatly tucked around her body, and a piece of black gauze cloth had been draped over her face. When Mrs Hill asked Ellison how anybody could have got into the house, he told her that 'they' had broken a window pane at the rear of the house, reached through and unlatched the window.

Ellison asked his neighbour to wait at the house while he went for the police. However, he took a most circuitous route. He first called at the home of another neighbour, Mrs Richards (who was Mrs Hill's mother), and told her that Mrs Seaman needed her at his house. From there, he went to the Temperance Hotel, where he told the landlord, Mr Thomas, about the murder and asked him to accompany him to the magistrate's home. After speaking to the magistrate, Mr Carne, Ellison then went to the Mayor of Penzance and once again related his story of an intruder breaking in and murdering 'poor Mrs Seaman'.

When the police began their investigations into the brutal slaying, it soon became obvious that Ellison's account of the murder did not add up. Mrs Seaman had last been seen alive watching the procession with Ellison, when she was wearing the same clothes in which she was dressed when her body was found. Upstairs, her nightclothes lay folded on her pillow and the bed obviously hadn't been slept in. There were a number of valuable items in the house and nothing seemed to be missing. This appeared to rule out burglary as a motive, although Ellison insisted that whoever had broken into the house had stolen several items of his clothing and also his watch.

Ellison told the police that an intruder had broken in through a sash window at the rear of the property. However, the only approach to that particular window was along a very wet and muddy lane. Both the internal and external walls of the house were painted white and a white deal table stood directly beneath the window, yet none showed any marks of mud.

A bloodstained axe was found in the next room, the size of which exactly corresponded with two large wounds in Mrs Seaman's head. Her skull was fractured beneath one of these wounds and according to surgeon Mitchell Thompson, who conducted the post-mortem examination, this was the injury that had proved fatal. In addition, Mrs Seaman's nose had been almost chopped from her face and she had numerous cuts on her chest, arms and hands. As the local paper was to report, '… her whole bust was almost one mass of livid bruises.' Thompson estimated that, when she was discovered, Mrs Seaman had been dead for at least twelve hours but probably much longer.

The police suspected that, rather than any intruder, Benjamin Ellison himself was Mrs Seaman's killer. A large clump of hair was clutched in each of the dead woman's hands. The brown hair in one hand was identical in colour to Ellison's hair and the grey hair in the other hand exactly matched his whiskers. Ellison's false teeth were found among the cold ashes in the fire grate.

The police traced Benjamin Ellison's movements in the hours before the murder was discovered. At between 1 p.m. and 2 p.m. on the afternoon of 7 July, Ellison called on Mr Richards, telling him that he was hoping to go into town to watch the festivities but had nobody to go with, since Mrs Seaman was too busy packing.
He next went to see Mr Glosson, to ask him if there was a meeting of the Temperance Society that evening. At that time, according to Mr Glosson, he appeared 'excited' and somewhat dishevelled in appearance.

Ellison then went to the Temperance Hotel for refreshments, drinking cocoa and eating cake in what was known as the smoking room. He was carrying a bundle beneath his arm but was seen during the evening by Mrs Elizabeth Bramble, carrying it towards the beach and, by the time he returned to the hotel much later, he no longer had his bundle with him. A witness saw him close to his home at around seven o'clock that evening and he visited Mr Richards again at nine o'clock, leaving after half an hour and returning to the hotel. There he asked the landlord if he could book a room for the night, saying that it was past ten o'clock and he didn't like to go home that late. Mr Thomas obliged him with a bed and he spent the night at the hotel, rising early the following morning and asking the landlord's son to clean his boots, which were very wet and muddy. The boy observed that Ellison was wearing a clean shirt, although no dirty laundry at all was found when his home was later searched.

Before going home on 8 July, he called at the barber's shop and asked for a haircut and for his whiskers to be trimmed. The barber, Mr Matthews, noted that parts of Ellison's hair had recently been clumsily chopped, obviously by a person who had no training as a hairdresser.

Witnesses who had seen Ellison on 7 July recalled that he was wearing a particular coat, of which there was no trace when the police searched the house after the discovery of Mrs Seaman's body. The police advertised a reward of 5s for anyone who found it and, on the Thursday after the murder, they were approached by Mr Jasper, who made his living as a rag picker. Jasper told them that he had been passing a dung heap close to the beach in Penzance and had seen some clothes concealed there, eventually recovering a torn coat, part of a pair of trousers, a waistcoat, a shirt, a pair of drawers and some stockings. Jasper had washed all the garments after finding them but the coat was missing a button and part of a second button, which were later found in the room where Mrs Seaman's body was discovered.

Ellison was arrested on suspicion of having murdered Mrs Seaman and denied everything. However, the police noticed on his arrest that he had fresh scratches on his face and a recent injury to his thumb that had every appearance of a human bite mark.

He continued to deny any knowledge of the murder, sticking rigidly to his story of an intruder entering the house while he was away for the night at the Temperance

Hotel. He insisted that the death of Mrs Seaman was financially ruinous for him, telling the police that she was about to be married to a man of great wealth and that she had promised to take care of him for the rest of his life. Confronted with the hair found clutched in Mrs Seaman's fists, he conceded that it did look very similar to his own but pointed out that it was much longer than his hair. He neglected to mention that he had visited the barber on the morning of 8 July, when the barber was forced to cut his hair very short to rectify the very amateurish attempt that somebody had recently made to trim it.

Ellison insisted that some of his clothes and his watch had been stolen from the house when Mrs Seaman was murdered. Yet the circumstantial evidence seemed to indicate that, on the night of the murder, he had been carrying the clothes around with him in a bundle and had disposed of them himself, concealing them in the dung heap by the beach. When the police questioned Ellison's neighbours, they discovered that he had recently given his watch to Mr Richards as security against a loan of 50s.

An inquest was opened into Mrs Seaman's death by borough coroner John Roscorla. It proved almost impossible to determine the exact nature of the relationship between the deceased and Benjamin Ellison, given that she had always referred to him as 'cousin', most probably for the sake of propriety. Rumours and gossip were rife within the town. Some people had heard of Mrs Seaman's impending marriage to a wealthy gentleman and others insisted that a number of love letters between her and Ellison had been found at the cottage, which, according to the local newspapers, were written with '... all the amorous enthusiasm of a lovelorn youth addressing some miss in her teens.'

Ellison's very identity was under question. He was thought by some to be an ex-militia man and by others to have connections with both manufacturing and property in the Halifax and Leeds areas of Yorkshire. All that was known for certain was that he had been sharing Mrs Seaman's home at the time of her death, even though he apparently already had a wife and children in Yorkshire, who he had abandoned six years previously. It was also suggested that, while living with Mrs Seaman, he frequently received items of mail addressed to at least two different names.

The inquest jury eventually returned a verdict of 'wilful murder' against Benjamin Ellison, who was committed to stand trial on a coroner's warrant. The proceedings opened before Mr Justice Erle at Bodmin on 30 July 1845. By six o'clock that morning, a massive crowd had assembled outside the court, hoping to be admitted to watch the proceedings. When the doors finally opened, the reporter from *The Times* compared the stampede to get into the building to 'bullock driving at Smithfield'. The javelin-men bellowed 'Keep back!' and 'Make way!' but their efforts to repel the crowd were fruitless as people pressed forward, determined to gain admittance to the courtroom by whatever means. The reporter himself only got inside with difficulty and, on entering the courtroom, immediately noticed that one corner of the gallery had given way and was in danger of plummeting into the main courtroom.

When the court officials tried to clear the gallery, they were met with great resistance – those who had battled their way into the room were not about to relinquish their places without a fight. Some clung to the railings and refused to let go and several women fainted. The court was eventually cleared in time for the trial to begin at 9 a.m., but by then the crowd outside was so dense that the judge was unable to get into the court. His path was cleared by the javelin-men, who then faced the same difficulty escorting the members of the jury into the room.

The prosecution counsel outlined the facts of the case for the jury, telling them that they needed to address two questions in particular. The first was when the murder was committed and the second, by whose hand.

The surgeon, said the prosecution counsel, was of the opinion that Mrs Seaman died at some time on 7 July. Hers was a terraced property and the party walls with the houses on either side were very thin. Had there been any noise from Mrs Seaman's property on the evening or night of 7 July, or on the morning of 8 July, it was impossible for her neighbours not to have heard it. Thus, it seemed most probable that the murder had been committed around midday on 7 July, at the time when the noise of gunshots from the celebrations in the town would have masked any sound from within the house. A witness had stated that she had heard 'fearful, dreadful, horrid groans' at around midday and the prosecution suggested that what she had actually heard was Mrs Seaman being brutally murdered.

Ellison's behaviour after this time had been most unusual. He had spoken to his neighbour, telling him that Mrs Seaman was too busy packing to accompany him to the festivities. Later that day, for the first time ever, he had booked a room for the night at the Temperance Hotel. William Eddy, an acquaintance of Ellison's, spoke with him at the hotel after being specifically told that Ellison wished to say something important to him. However, Ellison appeared extremely anxious and was completely unable to tell Eddy why he had asked to speak to him. When the two men took their leave of each other, Eddy held out his hand for Ellison to shake, which he declined to do.

Ellison had insisted all along to the police that his watch and some of his clothes had been stolen, although the police had found absolutely nothing to suggest that anyone had ever broken into the house and several items of value were left untouched. The police had then discovered that he had given his watch to Mr Richards and that he had been seen carrying a bundle towards the beach where his clothes were eventually found. There was also the matter of the hair in the dead woman's hands and Ellison's failure to tell the police that he had visited his barber immediately before finding Mrs Seaman dead. The prosecution also pointed out that a more normal reaction to finding the woman you were supposed to love dead would have been to call for help immediately rather than waiting half an hour. The axe in Mrs Seaman's kitchen was obviously the murder weapon and there was evidence that it had been washed after use, although not very thoroughly.

The case for the prosecution seemed watertight but Ellison's defence counsel addressed the jury on his client's behalf, reminding them that this was a capital case and that Ellison's life depended on their verdict. He asked them to dismiss everything they might have heard about the case prior to coming to court and to give the defendant the benefit of any doubts they might have.

He was accused of a 'foul and malicious murder' with no conceivable motive, having always been on the kindest, most affectionate terms with the victim. There was no jealousy or other ill-feeling between them and yet the prosecution were asking the jury to believe that Ellison had simply killed Mrs Seaman in cold blood, even though there was absolutely no proof that they had lived together as man and wife. The evidence pointed to the act being committed by a frenzied man, suggesting that there had been some argument between Ellison and his victim which, in the eyes of the law, would amount to provocation and so merit a reduction of the charge against his client from murder to manslaughter.

After Mr Justice Erle's summary of the case, the jury retired, needing only ten minutes of deliberation to return a verdict of 'Guilty of wilful murder' against Benjamin Ellison.

'Might I speak?' asked Ellison and, when given permission, he proceeded to talk at some length, referring constantly to the notes he had taken during his trial and pointing out what he believed were discrepancies in the evidence of those witnesses who had testified against him.

His voice barely faltered during his speech but it was to no avail as, as soon as he had finished speaking, Mr Justice Erle put on his black cap and sentenced him to death.

Sent to Bodmin Gaol to await his execution, Ellison apparently maintained his calm demeanour and military bearing to the end. There are conflicting reports in the contemporary newspapers about whether or not he eventually confessed his guilt, with some newspapers stating that he made no confession and others hinting that he had admitted killing Mrs Seaman in a letter written to a Penzance resident, possibly William Eddy. Regardless of whether or not he ever admitted his guilt, Ellison faced the executioner on 11 August 1845 with great courage. 'You have your job to do,' he told the executioner, as he was being prepared for the gallows, before helpfully pointing out that his wrist strap was too loose and asking the executioner to move his coat and shirt collar as they were in the way.

Having marched resolutely to the drop, Ellison occupied his last few minutes with prayer. Watched by a crowd of between 20-25,000 people, the hangman released the trap doors, leaving Ellison suspended motionless on the end of the rope. Yet, after hanging for five minutes, he suddenly began to struggle violently and it was a further three minutes before his frantic movements ceased entirely.

In the aftermath of the execution, it was reported that the executioner sold short lengths of the rope for 1s each. They were in great demand, since they were believed to cure such ailments as fits and king's evil (scrofula). It was also reported that William Hore, one of the spectators at the execution, was himself murdered on his way home to Fowey, being found in the parish of Lanlivery with the back of his head completely shattered.

8

'I WILL SCAT YOUR DAMNED OLD BRAINS ABOUT'

St Mabyn, 1846

After Samuel Hockin of St Mabyn was widowed, he began a passionate relationship with Mary Treverton, who was twenty years younger than him. Mary lived with her parents in the village but eventually moved into Samuel's home on the understanding that they would marry. However, in January 1846, Samuel suddenly announced that he was intending to marry another young woman, Ann, and that she had already given birth to his child about a year earlier.

Understandably, Mary Treverton was both hurt and furious. A violent quarrel ensued between her and Samuel, during which Mary told him, 'I will scat your damned old brains about', and immediately tried to make good her threat by hitting him over the head with an iron milk pan, cutting him badly.

Yet, within minutes, Samuel and Mary made up their differences and drank tea together. Samuel spent the night with Mary, before marrying Ann the next morning. As he walked up the road with his new bride, Mary was waiting for them and picked up handfuls of mud, which she threw at the newlyweds. Later that day she went into Hockin's house, emerging with her apron full of chair legs, and headed off in search of her errant lover.

When she finally located him, she first threw a couple of the chair legs at his head and, when Samuel tried to run away, she chased after him, belabouring his back with a third. Samuel ran, trying to escape, until he got as far as Mary's house, where he suddenly stopped and turned to face her. Much to the amusement of bystanders, Mary dealt a series of blows to Samuel's head. 'Knock her down,' the onlookers urged. 'Don't just stand there having your brains beaten out.' Samuel probably felt that he deserved some of the punishment that Mary was dishing out, since, although he picked up one of the chair legs, he took the blows without raising a hand to her. Eventually, Mary's mother, Ann, came out of her house and ordered her daughter inside, thus ending the fight before too much blood could be spilled. Samuel obviously still cared for Mary as, after just three weeks of marriage, he left his wife and went back to her, taking lodgings with her away from St Mabyn.

Three weeks later, he was back with his wife again. Yet he seemed unable to give up his association with Mary and visited her constantly, even spending occasional nights in her bed.

Not surprisingly, his new wife was most unhappy with this state of affairs and eventually gave Samuel an ultimatum – he must end his affair with Mary Treverton immediately. Faced with his wife's wrath, Samuel finally promised to break off all contact with his former partner of four years and, once again, Mary was angered by his desertion of her, taking every possible opportunity to swear at Hockin and telling anyone who would listen to her that she would like to 'scatter his brains'. On one occasion, in front of Hockin's son from his first marriage, Mary threatened, 'I'll blow thee and thy wife's brains out with gunpowder if there's any to be got this night between this and Bodmin.'

On Saturday, 10 October 1846, at just before six o'clock in the morning, John Clements was walking along Denham Bridge Lane, when he stumbled over a man lying on his side on the road, his head propped up against the wall of the cottage. He was obviously dreadfully hurt. Clements immediately roused nearby residents Mr and Mrs Perry and, while William Perry hurried to fetch the village surgeon, Mr Arthur Gaved, Mrs Perry went back with Clements to try and administer first aid.

Gaved was on the scene within minutes, finding the man unconscious but still breathing, although heavily and erratically. By now a crowd had gathered, and the victim was soon recognised as Samuel Hockin. On Mr Gaved's instructions, he was carried to his house but sadly died shortly after arriving home. When Gaved later conducted a post-mortem examination, he found that Hockin's light fustian coat was torn in several places, as if he had engaged in a scuffle before his death, and his pockets were turned out. He had a massive skull fracture, some 5in long, on the right-hand side of the back of his head, with severe damage to his brain beneath it. In addition, Hockin's eyes were swollen almost shut and he had a large cut on his temple, again with a corresponding skull fracture, as well as several other cuts and bruises on his head and face.

With the arrival of daylight, it was possible to see spatters of blood and brain matter on the wall of the cottage, against which Hockin was found leaning. Hockin's hat and a pipe were found just feet from where he had fallen, the pipe still half-filled with tobacco as if it had been knocked from Hockin's mouth when he was attacked. Less than 6ft away was a large, pointed stone, roughly half the size of a man's head which, since it still bore fresh bloodstains and strands of human hair, was obviously the murder weapon.

County magistrates William and Francis John Hext began to make enquiries into the murder and, as a starting point, tried to trace Hockin's movements immediately before his death. He had left his home at about seven o'clock in the evening and the magistrates soon discovered that the last place he was seen alive was at the home of Mary Treverton and her parents. Hockin had visited Mary's home on the evening prior to his death and, at about ten o'clock that night, Mary Treverton had left the house, shortly to be followed by Samuel Hockin.

Mary Dart, who lived close to the Trevertons' house, had argued with her husband, Philip, that evening and, as a consequence, had refused to join him in their marital bed. Instead, she sat brooding by her kitchen fire all night. While the inside of her house was in darkness, apart from the firelight, outside it was a bright, moonlit night and, as she gazed out of her window onto the street, Mrs Dart had a clear view of everything that happened outside.

Mrs Dart told the magistrates that, at about 1 a.m., she saw a light in the kitchen of the Trevertons' house and between two and three o'clock she twice saw a man walking past her window. He headed first away from and then, ten minutes later, back towards the Trevertons' home. Mary Dart said that she believed the man she had seen was Samuel Hockin.

Shortly after five o'clock in the morning, Mary Dart went to the Trevertons' house and knocked on the door. She heard Mr Treverton shout from upstairs and, a few minutes later, Mary Treverton came to the door, fully dressed with the exception of her shoes. Mary Dart jokingly asked Mary Treverton if she had been to bed with all her clothes on, but Mary replied that she had just dressed. She was carrying a chamber pot and went outside to empty it, after which she busied herself lighting the fire.

Denham / Dinham Bridge, St Mabyn. (© N. Sly)

As the two women sat chatting, they heard noises from the street. 'Hark, what's that?' Mary Treverton asked, crossing to the window. Moments later, Mary Dart's young daughter burst into the house with the news that Samuel Hockin had been found murdered and his brains had been 'knocked out'.

'Who could be so cruel?' asked Mary Treverton.

Mary Dart asked her if she wanted to go outside and see what was happening but Mary Treverton demurred, saying that she couldn't bear to look. Mary Dart opened the cottage door at which George Stephens, one of the neighbours, told her that the nearby houses were being searched. 'You may depend on it, the house will be searched in a minute,' said Stephens and, on hearing this, Mary Treverton jumped to her feet and ran upstairs, not coming down again until Joseph West, the village constable, arrived.

As West entered the communal passage that ran between the Trevertons' house and that of their neighbours, the Ham family, he noticed a small spot of blood on the doorpost, near the thumb latch. Having discovered that the dead man had apparently visited the Trevertons' home before he died, West arrested the entire family and took them to the village pub, securely locking the house before he left. He returned soon afterwards with Mr Gaved and began a search of the house where, under the mattress on Mary Treverton's bed, they found a pair of very wet, dirty shoes, which appeared to be spotted with blood. West and Gaved made a cursory examination of the shoes, from which they determined that one seemed to have been recently wiped. They then took them to the pub, where they were placed on a table.

'They have found her shoes with blood on them and that will hang her,' somebody commented in Mary Treverton's hearing. Mary immediately turned to her mother, saying, 'You can clear me of that,' apparently referring to what the newspapers of the time called a 'periodical illness'.

The shoes lay ignored on the table until the inquest, when the coroner suggested that they should be more closely examined. 'Any reasonable person would have done that in the first instance,' bemoaned the contemporary newspapers and, indeed, when Gaved and West closely inspected the shoes, several strands of human hair were found stuck to them. However, as the coroner pointed out, in consequence of the stupidity of Gaved and West in not carefully examining the shoes when they were first found, and subsequently leaving them unattended on a table in the pub, the chain of evidence was broken and the discovery of the hair was worthless. Since Mary Treverton maintained that the blood was menstrual, the coroner ordered Mr Gaved to examine her to determine whether or not she was menstruating. Gaved found no staining on her underclothes but reported that she may have been 'in the state alluded to' at the time of the murder, since he found some stains on her outer garments.

Thus, in spite of the fact that the fiery relationship between the victim and Mary Treverton was fully explained at the inquest, the coroner's jury returned a verdict of 'murder by person or persons unknown'.

The magistrates continued to investigate the case, taking statements from a number of witnesses. Since all the evidence seemed to point to Mary Treverton as Hockin's killer, she was eventually brought before them and confronted with the statements made against her. Asked if she wanted to question the witnesses, she declined and, although there was no concrete evidence to connect her with the murder, the magistrates determined that there was sufficient circumstantial evidence to charge her.

Mary Treverton stood trial at Bodmin Assizes before Mr Justice Cresswell on 29 March 1847. The prosecutors were Mr Rowe and Mr Cornish, while Mary was defended by Mr Slade.

Mary Treverton was described in the contemporary newspapers as '... a large woman, of strong and masculine appearance and coarse exterior'. Nevertheless, she wept as she pleaded 'Not Guilty' to the charge against her, that she had wilfully murdered Samuel Hockin 'by striking and beating him with a stone upon the head, thereby giving him diverse mortal wounds and diverse fractures of the skull whereof he died.'

For the prosecution, the crux of the case was the stormy relationship between Mary Treverton and Samuel Hockin. Fully expecting marriage, Mary had been spurned by Samuel who had then vacillated between her and his wife, as and when the fancy took him. Faced with an ultimatum from Ann, Samuel had chosen her above Mary, leaving Mary hurt, jealous, angry and, according to the prosecution, vengeful.

Mr Rowe called several witnesses who had either seen physical fights between Samuel and Mary or heard her making threats of violence towards him.

Mr Gaved was called to testify about tending to Samuel Hockin on 10 October and to detail his findings at the subsequent post-mortem examination. The large stone found near Hockin was produced in court as evidence and Gaved stated that it could have caused the wounds he had observed on Hockin's head, denying under cross-examination that the dead man's injuries could have resulted from a fall.

Gaved was then asked about the shoes found under Mary Treverton's bed shortly after the murder. He told the court that he had been present when Joseph West searched the house. There had been two beds in the bedroom, one of which was shared by John Treverton, his wife and their five-year-old granddaughter (who was Mary's sister Jane's child), and another which Mary slept in.

Mary's bed had two chaff mattresses, between which the shoes had been concealed. Gaved stated that the shoes were wet when found and the right shoe appeared to have been scraped or wiped with something rough. The left shoe, which had not been wiped, was very dirty. There were several small spots of blood on the right shoe, the largest of which was about half an inch in diameter. West had taken possession of the shoes, after which Gaved had not seen them again until the day of the inquest, when he saw four or five hairs trapped between the sole and the upper leather.

The coroner had ordered him to preserve the hairs, so he had removed them from the shoe and wrapped them in a piece of paper. Later that day, he had removed some hair from Samuel's head for comparison, which he presented to Joseph West.

Gaved was then cross-examined by Mr Slade about Mary Treverton's menstrual cycle and Gaved answered Slade's questions by admitting that Mary could have been menstruating on the day of the murder.

Hockin's widow, Ann, was called into the witness box to describe the complex relationship between herself, her husband and his former partner. She related going to Mary Treverton's home in search of her husband on more than one occasion and, once, five or six weeks before his death, engaging in a tug-of-war on Mary's doorstep, with Mary trying to pull Samuel inside, while she tried equally hard to pull him away. 'He was continually going to Mary Treverton's up to the time of his death,' Ann stated.

George Stephens agreed with her, saying that he had frequently seen Hockin at Mary's house, the last occasion being on the night of 9 October, shortly before his death. Stephens stated that on that night, Samuel and Mary appeared to be good friends and seemed very fond of each other, although Hockin appeared to have been drinking.

The prosecution then called Mary Pooley, who lived in St Mabyn and could see the spot where the body was found from her bedroom window. Mrs Pooley was wakened at about four o'clock on the morning of 10 October by a scuffle taking place outside her house. She had known Samuel Hockin for many years and quite clearly recognised his voice saying, 'Let me go' – a phrase he repeated a few moments later from further on along the road, towards the place where his body was eventually found.

She had distinctly heard a second person speaking, although she didn't recognise that voice, saying that it was an 'undertone'. Then, a few minutes later, she had heard running footsteps going in the direction of the Trevertons' house. 'It was neither a light nor a heavy step,' she stated, adding that she had heard no cry or scream – nothing apart from the two voices.

Mrs Jane Ham lived next door to the Trevertons, their bedrooms separated by only a thin partition wall. On the night of 9/10 October, Jane Ham's child was ill and, as a result, she had slept only fitfully. Called as a prosecution witness, Mrs Ham said that, throughout the night, she had heard several voices next door and had also frequently heard the door of the communal passage opening and closing. The last time had been at about four o'clock in the morning, when someone walked by her window, opened the passage door and then apparently walked upstairs in the Trevertons' house.

Under cross-examination, Mrs Ham stressed that it had been the passage door she had heard opening and closing during the night, not the door leading into her neighbours' house.

William Harris had also been awake at four o'clock in the morning and he too had heard running footsteps approaching the Trevertons' house and entering the passageway. He got out of bed and looked out of the window but, in spite of the bright moonlight, he saw nobody.

Mary's father, John Treverton, told the court that he had felt unwell on 9 October and consequently went to bed at seven o'clock in the evening, although he was unable to sleep and spent most of the night tossing and turning. There were two beds in the bedroom and both Mary and her mother had been in bed well before midnight. John Treverton swore that his daughter did not leave the bedroom at any time after retiring until Mary Dart arrived, at which he saw his daughter get up and get dressed, leaving the room carrying the chamber pot.

John said that he had heard Samuel Hockin downstairs on the night of 9 October. 'There was no keeping him away,' he said ruefully, adding that he had heard Hockin saying 'Good night' at about half-past eleven, after which Mary immediately went to bed.

Shown the shoes found hidden between Mary's mattresses, John said that they did not belong to him or his wife but he didn't know if they belonged to his daughter or not. 'I never took any notice of her shoes,' he stated, admitting that he had no idea how many pairs of shoes his daughter owned.

Neighbour George Stephens was then recalled. He was a shoemaker and, unlike John Treverton, always took notice of people's footwear. Stephens testified to the fact that Mary Treverton owned an identical pair of shoes, after which another shoemaker, John Bligh, took the stand and testified to having made that particular pair for her.

When the prosecution rested, it was the turn of Mr Slade to speak in defence of Mary Treverton. He admitted that she and Samuel had quarrelled frequently, but insisted that they loved each other and that Mary had never entertained any ideas of killing him. In the light of Hockin's callous treatment of her, said Slade, it was hardly surprising that they should quarrel and it was common for people who were angry to use coarse and revolting language.

Slade reminded the jury that Mrs Pooley had recognised Samuel Hockin's voice and that the person he was addressing at the time had responded in an 'undertone'. Had that person been Mary Treverton, she would doubtless have been angry with the deceased and would more probably have shouted than spoken quietly. Mrs Pooley had known Mary Treverton for many years and yet had not recognised her voice.

Several people had heard someone entering the passage beside the Trevertons' house at four o'clock in the morning. Anyone who had just murdered Hockin and knew the area could have been that person, since by cutting through the back garden they would reach the fields behind the house, that being the quickest and most convenient escape route.

Mary might have been angry with Samuel Hockin, although George Stephens had testified that they were getting on very well together just hours before the murder. Even if she was angry, she had no reason to tear his coat or to turn out his coat pockets, which seemed to indicate that he had been robbed.

Although Samuel Hockin smoked, nobody had been able to identify the pipe found near his body as belonging to him. Was it not possible, Slade asked, that the pipe belonged to his assailant?

Slade reminded the jury that Mary's father had reportedly lain awake, feeling ill, for most of the night of 9/10 October and had sworn under oath that Mary had never left the bedroom until Mary Dart came to call.

Next, Slade addressed the matter of the shoes. Although the prosecution had the hairs taken from the shoes and the hairs from the deceased's head in court, they had been unable to introduce them as evidence due to the laxity of Gaved and West in not examining them properly and leaving them unattended on a table in the pub. The shoes were very down at heel and Slade questioned whether Mary would have been able to run in them – given the state of the shoes, could the running footsteps described by the witnesses have been hers? Admittedly, her shoes were both damp and dirty but that was hardly surprising, given the weather on the day before the murder, and it was not unreasonable to suppose that, if her shoes got wet and muddy, she would have wiped them.

It emerged in court that the large stone, believed to have been the murder weapon, had been passed around between several people, before finally being handed to Constable West. Although blood and brain tissue had liberally spattered the walls of the cottage where Samuel Hockin had been found, to a height of 5ft, no trace of either blood or brain matter had been found on Mary Treverton's clothes, save for some small spots on her shoes and some smears on her outer clothing, all of which could be attributed to menstrual blood.

Slade concluded his speech by telling the jury that, in order to find Mary Treverton guilty, they must satisfy themselves of the facts of the case as clearly as if they had seen her strike the fatal blow with their own eyes. Before sitting down, he urged the jury to acquit his client.

Mr Justice Cresswell's summary of the evidence for the jury appeared strongly biased in favour of the defendant and thus it came as no surprise to anyone in court when, after deliberating for just ten minutes, the jury answered Mr Slade's plea and acquitted Mary Treverton.

On hearing the verdict, Mary clapped her hands in delight and laughed out loud, then immediately burst into tears. She walked from the court a free woman.

Nobody else was ever charged with Samuel Hockin's murder, which remains unsolved to this day.

Note: Samuel Hockin's name is also recorded as Hocking in some contemporary accounts of the murder.

9

'I BELIEVE PHILIPPA IS DEAD!'

In 1847 James Holman, a labourer who lived about half a mile from Redruth, married Philippa Parkin, daughter of a farmer at Gwinear. At the time, she was eighteen and he was about six years older. It was not a match that met with the approval of her family, who considered her too good for him. Within the next four years the couple moved into the parish of Sithney and had two children, a girl born about a year after the marriage and a son two years later. When problems between them developed, James left the family and went to Wales, where he stayed on his own for two and a half years. Early in 1853 he returned to Cornwall, evidently keen to make a new start with them, and they moved to a farm at Carne in Crowan. It was in a very secluded spot, with only two neighbouring families, Roberts and Williams, who both lived within about fifty yards or so. Mr Williams was Mr Roberts's son-in-law.

James Holman had a reputation for being reserved and keeping very much to himself. Philippa was better liked, and everybody knew her as a hardworking but cheerful and industrious young woman.

On 1 December 1853, James Holman visited his father-in-law, Mr Parkin, to make enquiries about buying some pigs. Philippa's seventeen-year-old sister Elizabeth was there, and she asked her brother-in-law how Philippa was. He said that she was very poorly, and had been so for some time. A gravely concerned Mrs Parkin questioned him further, and he told her sadly that she was fading fast. As Philippa Holman was known to be expecting another baby in two or three months, and as she had seemed in good health the last time they had seen her, they were very worried.

After dinner that evening Elizabeth went out into the fields, and James followed her. He put his arm around her and told her that she was going to be his next wife. When she told him that he had a wife already, he repeated that he did not expect her to live long, and asked her whether she would wait twelve months for him. Try as she would to change the subject of the conversation, he persisted in asking her whether she would wait for him. She said that her sister might live as long as both of them, and James then suggested that Elizabeth herself might die before he did. Rather incongruously, he followed this by telling her that he had planned for them to be married at Gunwalloe church, after which he would take her to Wales for a spree in a steamer. Although she was wise enough to show him that she did not take the conversation seriously, she must have found it very unsettling.

As the Holmans had no servants, Philippa was kept busy much of the day working around the farm and cottage. When she was last seen alive on the afternoon of 26 December 1853, she seemed in perfect health and spirits.

At about nine o'clock that evening Mr Holman met two of the Roberts boys climbing over a stile on their way home, and asked if their father was in. They said they believed he was, and Holman ran to the house, calling out, 'Roberts, come down; I believe Philippa is dead!' Roberts had just gone to bed. Thoroughly alarmed, he threw on his clothes, came down, collected Williams, and they all went back to Holman's cottage.

There they found Philippa Holman lying dead under the grate, her face covered with blood and ashes. A lighted candle was in the ashes, with rags around the bottom, and this was the only light in the house. On her left was a flat round iron, and a brandis, or baking kettle. There were spots of blood around the house in various places, especially the walls, and on a stool under the table. Her hands and some of her clothes were badly burned.

Roberts and Williams carried her upstairs, and when Williams washed her face, deep wounds over the temple and nose were visible. The skull was broken in several places, while her nose and the upper parts of her body also bore marks of violence. There was blood on the sleeve of Holman's coat and trousers under the knee.

Gwinear. (© N. Sly)

When one of Philippa's brothers came to see his sister's body, Holman would not allow him in, and the former had to force an entrance. To family and friends, the widower seemed to be trying to cover things up. He did not appear grief-stricken, and his statements were often contradictory. To his mother-in-law, he said that there could not have been a better woman. Another person was told that Philippa was a habitual drunkard, but her family said that they had never seen her the worse for liquor.

The constable who was called in found blood on Holman's shirt, and asked him how it came to be there. He said that he must have rubbed against his wife when he lifted her up; all of his clothes which had bloodstains were then taken from him.

An inquest was held on 29 December, and the surgeons, Mr Gurney and his assistant Thomas Hutchinson, said they were satisfied that the injuries had not been caused merely by her falling over. At the post-mortem on the same day Gurney, who was sure that the deceased had been hit repeatedly with a hatchet, asked Holman if he kept such a weapon on the premises. Holman denied this, but nobody believed him.

Two days later, Constable John Webster went to search an 8ft deep well beside the cottage. He looked inside and saw something in the middle, and found a bloodstained hatchet. He took it into the house and asked Holman if it was his. Holman denied all knowledge of it, until one of the neighbours identified it as his property. Webster then took Holman into custody, and led him to Semmens's public house. Shortly after they arrived, the prisoner seemed very restless and alarmed about something. Webster and his colleague, Constable Philip Orchard, put handcuffs on him, and began questioning him. He said he did not see anything, but a few minutes later said he saw glittering swords and soldiers before his eyes. He started screaming, and Mr Semmens came in to see what was the matter.

Holman had evidently realised the game was up, and said he would tell Semmens 'the truth of it'. Semmens said he would not hear it, but was prepared to fetch somebody else. Holman then asked to see Richard Bryant, the foreman of the jury, and Thomas Symons, one of the other jurors. When they arrived, after he had been cautioned, he dictated a statement:

> I left home on Monday morning [26 December], and returned in the evening. As I came in I called out 'Philippa, where are you?' And she answered, 'What is that to you?' I then said, 'You are drunk again, I see'; upon hearing which she threw the hatchet at me. I then gave her a push, and she fell forward into the fireplace. I left her there, and went out to feed the cattle, but, finding her in the same position when I returned, I lifted her up, and found her dead, with a cut over the forehead. I then saw the hatchet on the floor, covered with blood, and, fearing I might be suspected of murder, I took it away to throw it into the wall the next morning. I had not said anything about Philippa's getting drunk, to any person but Mr Trewhella [his brother-in-law]; that was about a month since. I did not murder her ...

[This confession was quoted in different publications, with slight variations in wording, but with the basic message and details being much the same in each.]

Afterwards, Symons read it out to him for his approval. He admitted that this was 'the truth of it', adding that if he was found guilty, 'I trust you will do your best to get me out on bail.' Holman evidently regarded the offence as manslaughter, hoping that the defence would make the most of this and argue that there had been a strong element of provocation on his wife's part.

He was charged with wilful murder, and went on trial at Bodmin on 25 March 1854 before Mr Baron Martin, pleading 'Not Guilty'. One of the first witnesses called was William Roberts, who said that after he arrived on the premises to find Philippa Holman dead, he asked Holman if anything had been stolen, and Holman admitted nothing had gone. He had often seen Philippa, and found her clever, likeable – and never once saw her drunk. The latter was confirmed by all other witnesses when questioned, some regarding the idea as extraordinary. It was apparent, or at least highly probable, that Holman had fabricated the statement in order to try and make himself appear less culpable.

Other witnesses included another local farmer, Thomas Cory, Philippa's brother John, her sister Elizabeth, the two constables, and Thomas Hutchinson, the surgeon. Mr Gurney had since died, but not before he had had an opportunity to make a deposition, which was given to the coroner.

The jury found Holman guilty of murder, and in passing the sentence of death the judge told him sternly that he had been convicted of the murder of the person whom above all others he was bound to cherish and protect. His statements about his wife having been drinking were patently untrue, and she had always been 'a perfectly sober woman'.

In accordance with general custom, two Sundays were allowed to elapse between the passing of the sentence and the execution. A petition pleading for mercy, on the grounds that he had not killed his wife from premeditation or malice aforethought, was circulated around Bodmin, but only attracted about 100 signatures. It was forwarded to the Home Secretary, Viscount Palmerston, who acknowledged it but replied that he saw no grounds to recommend that Her Majesty should interfere with the due course of the law in this particular case.

While he was in gaol, on the day after the trial, Elizabeth Parkin took his daughter in to see him for the last time. Greatly moved at the sight of her, he took her on his knee and wept profusely. When he was hanged on 3 April, the crowds who came to watch were denounced by a correspondent to the *West Briton*, who wrote indignantly that:

The majesty of the law has been once more avenged! Another great exhibition has been offered for the moral improvement and edification of the people! For the rejoicing or sorrow of a Christian nation, another immortal soul has been sent to heaven or to hell!! Calcraft, with a plenary indulgence and a foe, has dared in open day and in the face of an assembled multitude to repeat the crime of Holman; – to illustrate to the people the value and the sanctity of human life, human life has been taken. A nation under the sanction of the law (?) has done that which was intolerable in Holman as an individual.

10

THE CASE OF THE POISONED PASTY

Metherell, 1853

In July 1853 Caroline Pellow, aged six months, and her father Robert, a miner who lived at Metherell, near Harrowbarrow, were both taken ill with food poisoning. Robert soon recovered but his little daughter died. At first nobody had any reason to suppose that there was anything sinister about her death, and after the usual formalities she was laid to rest.

One month later her mother, thirty-year-old Eliza Pellow and William Tregay, their lodger, who was thought to be about a year younger, both suddenly disappeared. After this there were suspicions that Caroline might not have died of natural causes after all. The deputy coroner, Mr Hamlyn, was alerted, and on 24 August 1853 the body of Caroline was exhumed. An inquest was held, and it was proved by witnesses that Tregay had obtained poison for Mrs Pellow at various times. Not only had she eloped with him immediately after her daughter's death, but it was apparent that she had already tried to kill her husband by putting poison in a pasty she had prepared for him, and which he took to the mine when he went to work. He ate some, was violently sick, drank some warm salt and water and vomited up the rest. A dog belonging to a fellow miner had gobbled up the rest and died almost at once.

The enquiry was adjourned to await further medical evidence, which established that there had been enough arsenic in the baby's stomach to cause the deaths of three adults. A verdict of wilful murder was returned against Mrs Pellow, and a hunt was launched throughout the area. On 26 August she and Tregay were traced to a lodging house in St Austell and apprehended while they were in bed together. It was said to be the third time that Tregay had run off with somebody else's wife. Another child of the Pellows, a little less than two years old, was with them at the time, and was taken into care at the St Austell workhouse.

The authorities decided that Tregay was innocent. On 24 March 1854 Eliza Pellow alone stood trial at Bodmin Crown Court before Mr Justice Erle, charged with the murder of her baby daughter.

For the prosecution, Mr Gill said he did not intend to offer any evidence on this indictment. Addressing the jury, the judge said the matter of murder was investigated before the Grand Jury, who believed there was no case to find a bill that was likely to lead to a conviction. The learned counsel for the prosecution believed that public justice did not require them to go into the case. In that, he said he concurred, and therefore no evidence would be offered upon the charge. The jury would therefore be directed to return a verdict of 'Not Guilty'.

Eliza Pellow was then charged with feloniously administering to her husband six grains of arsenic. Mr Gill said that the evidence he would offer was not positive, but circumstantial. It would be for the jury to say whether it was sufficient for them to find her guilty on that indictment. He would show them that one morning she was seen making a pasty for the family to eat at dinner that night. She separated a certain amount from the rest, intending to give it to her husband, saying she wanted to put some more lard in it for him. The woman who witnessed this, probably a next-door neighbour, was then sent out of the room. By the time she came back the food had been cooked, and this was the portion her husband was given to eat.

While eating the food he offered to give some of it to their small daughter. Eliza told him not to do so as she would only waste it, and he had to eat it himself. After he had done so he was taken violently ill. When he recovered, he accused his wife of having put arsenic in his food, but she indignantly denied having done any such thing. He went out and she told the child to throw the rest of the pasty away in a field. If anybody was to ask her what she had done with it, she must tell them that she had eaten it herself. There was no way of proving that there had been any arsenic in the pasty.

The judge said he would never interfere by taking the matter out of the jury's hands. This charge was one of the utmost seriousness, and there had to be some way of proving it. As there was nothing to show what had caused the illness, he would ask the jury whether they would return a verdict of acquittal at once on the opening of the case, or whether they would wish that opening to be proved by evidence. For the second time that day, the jury said they were prepared to give a verdict of 'Not Guilty'.

The case history suggested that it was perfectly possible for Mrs Pellow to have killed her daughter, with Tregay acting as her accomplice. If this was so, then they had been very fortunate. Another jury might easily have taken a less lenient view and sent her to the gallows.

11

'THE TRUTH'S BAD ENOUGH BUT LIES ARE WORSE'

Near Probus, 1853

On 14 June 1853, licensed hawker William Measurer was travelling in the area around Truro and stopped to wait for his wife near the village of Probus. A clear mill stream ran a few yards from the roadside and, as he waited, it crossed Measurer's mind that there might be trout in it. He walked to the stream and knelt on the bank, but as he leaned over to peer into the water he got the shock of his life. Rather than the hoped-for fish supper, what Measurer found in the stream was the dead body of a young baby lying on its right side, completely underwater.

Measurer raised the alarm and waited by the stream until the village constable arrived from Probus and removed the baby's body, when it was noted that there was a clear imprint of the infant's arm in the clay at the bottom of the stream, as though the child had been pushed or weighted down in the water.

At a post-mortem examination the following day, surgeon John Paddon found no external marks of violence on the tiny body. The otherwise healthy baby boy, who Paddon estimated to be between six and eight weeks old, had died by drowning and, since there was no possible way that such a young child could have got into the water by itself, it was obvious that the baby had been murdered.

The police already had a good idea of the infant's identity since, on the day before the murder, a young woman with a baby had reported to the police station at Truro, saying that the child had been abandoned by his mother. Seventeen-year-old Jane Chenoweth was a former inmate of the Truro Union workhouse and while there she had befriended a single woman, Elizabeth Beard. On 7 May 1853, Elizabeth gave birth to an illegitimate baby, whom she named William.

Elizabeth already had one illegitimate child, who lived with her father. However, Elizabeth's father was a poor man, who struggled to make ends meet, and she was well aware that he would not be able to support a second 'mistake'. Thus, the only future that Elizabeth could see for herself was being sent to the workhouse hospital, where she would be expected to lay out the dead. To Elizabeth, this was a vision that filled her with terror.

On 10 June, she left the workhouse with baby William and walked to her home in Probus. As she had anticipated, her father was not overjoyed to see her with another baby in her arms and, after spending the weekend at home, Elizabeth took William to a lodging house in Calenick Street in Truro, where she met up with Jane Chenoweth.

Elizabeth asked Jane if she would mind watching the baby while she went to get something to eat and, when Jane agreed, she wrapped William in her green worsted shawl and placed him on Jane's lap. In Truro, Elizabeth bought a loaf of bread, which she gave to a woman she met in the street, asking her to take it to the lodging house. Then Elizabeth just kept on walking back to her home in Probus, leaving Jane Chenoweth literally holding the baby.

When his mother did not return, Jane took baby William to the police station at Truro, where she spoke to Inspector William J. Nash, telling him that Elizabeth Beard had abandoned her child. Nash advised her to take the baby to the Union, but an hour later Jane was back at the police station, still carrying William.

Probus. (Authors' collection)

She told Nash that the officers at the workhouse would not admit the baby without an official order from the parish. Nash directed her to a parish overseer, who supplied the necessary paperwork but, by the time Jane arrived at the workhouse again, it was almost nine o'clock at night and, although she rang the bell outside several times for admittance, nobody came to let her in.

Jane went back to the police station for the third time to tell Nash that she had been unable to leave the baby at the workhouse. Nash gave her a shilling and told her to take the infant to the lodging house for the night and to return to the police station at nine o'clock the next morning, when he would accompany her to the Union and see that the baby was admitted.

When Jane did not appear with the baby at the appointed time, Nash instructed a constable to go to Probus and arrest Elizabeth Beard for deserting her child. She was brought to the police station in Truro and questioned, but was discharged by the mayor later that afternoon and walked back to Probus. By the time she arrived there, the baby's body had already been found and taken to the nearby Wheel Inn. Elizabeth was able to identify her son, after which she was arrested yet again and taken back to the police station at Truro.

Meanwhile, the police began a search for Jane Chenoweth, starting in the village of Probus. They found three witnesses who had seen Jane on the afternoon of 14 June. Ann Nobble, who lived in a cottage near Probus, was friendly with Elizabeth Beard and had seen a woman carrying a baby walking past her cottage between midday and one o'clock. Elizabeth had visited Mrs Nobble with William only the previous day and consequently Mrs Nobble recognised the shawl that the baby was wrapped in as the one she had so recently seen in Elizabeth's possession.

Mrs Nobble sent her daughter, Emma, to fetch the woman and Emma caught up with her by the stream, where the woman was kneeling to drink. The baby was crying lustily and the young woman angrily jerked it to her breast, telling it to be quiet. The woman declined to come into the Nobbles' cottage and, having quenched her thirst, set off towards Probus. She was seen shortly afterwards by Robert May, who was drinking at the New Inn at Tresillian Bridge, by which time she was no longer carrying a baby.

May told the police that Jane Chenoweth was heading towards Bodmin when he last saw her and Constable John Fuddler set off in pursuit. He caught up with her about eighteen miles outside Truro and transported her back to the New Inn, where he placed her in the custody of Constable John Hugo until arrangements could be made to take her to Bodmin.

As Fuddler and Jane breakfasted at the inn the next morning, landlady Maria Cook asked her, 'How could you have the heart to put the stone on the child's head?'

'I did not,' replied Jane.

'How in the world could you ever have the heart to drown the child?' Mrs Cook persisted.

'The child was very cross and I was tired and when I came there I dabbed it down in the mud and water and went away and left it,' Jane admitted.

Tresillian Bridge and church. (Authors' collection)

The police made arrangements with John Pearce, a printer from London who happened to be visiting the area, to take Jane to Bodmin Gaol in his carriage. Like Maria Cook, Pearce was interested in Jane's motive for killing such a young baby. He noticed that, when they neared Probus, Jane pulled aside the curtains at the carriage windows and, when he asked her what she was looking at, she told him that she wanted to see the place where the baby drowned.

'How do you know where the baby drowned?' Pearce asked, but Jane did not reply.

She repeated what she had said to Maria Cook about the baby crying all the way from Truro.

'I'm afraid it is a very bad case, especially if what people say is true – that you held the child down until it was dead,' said Pearce.

'That is not true. It is a lie,' Jane replied indignantly. 'I threw the child in the leat and went away.'

'Did you throw it in, or put it in?' asked Pearce.

'I went to the water's edge, put the child in and went on my way,' Jane explained.

Jane Chenoweth's trial for the wilful murder of William Beard opened at Bodmin Assizes on 27 July 1853, before Mr Justice Talfourd. Mr Stock acted for the prosecution and, at the judge's request, Mr Bevan agreed to undertake Jane's defence.

The first witness was Elizabeth Beard, who assured the court 'I was very fond of my child.' She admitted to abandoning William, saying that she could not afford to keep him and had fully expected Jane to take him back to the workhouse when she didn't return to collect him.

Inspector Nash described Jane's unsuccessful efforts to do just that, admitting that she seemed very attentive and caring towards baby William. Jane sobbed in the dock as Nash gave his evidence, before shouting out that he had not given her a shilling to take the baby back to her lodgings. 'The truth's bad enough but lies are worse,' she complained.

Ann and Emma Nobble and Robert May testified to seeing Jane near Probus on the afternoon of the murder, first carrying a baby and then alone. In her original statement to the police, Emma Nobble had described Jane as acting 'angrily' towards baby William, saying that she had been 'in a passion' when she jerked the crying child up against her. Under cross-examination by counsel for the defence, she now admitted that she had seen her own mother 'hush' her little brothers and sisters in exactly the same manner.

William Measurer described finding William's tiny body in the stream, telling the court that the impression of the body in the mud seemed to indicate that the child had been pressed down hard into the stream bed. Surgeon John Paddon detailed the results of the post-mortem examination, reiterating the fact that the infant had been immersed in water during life, although he had found no marks of violence on his body.

PC Fuddler and Maria Cook recalled Jane's overnight stay at the New Inn, both testifying that she had confessed to 'dabbing' the baby in the water and then walking away. John Pearce gave a similar account of Jane's statements during the drive to Bodmin Gaol, although Jane insisted tearfully from the dock that he was 'speaking false' against her. 'She did not appear in the least degree agitated,' stated Pearce and then, over Jane's protests, he continued to say that, during the journey, Jane informed him that she had seen his carriage on the road on the day after the murder and asked him if he had noticed her.

Pearce said he thought he might have done but was not absolutely sure. 'I don't think you did, as I endeavoured to shun your car,' Jane said and, when Pearce asked her why she had tried to avoid being seen, she told him that she was worried he might have heard about the baby and that he would 'put the constable on the track I was going.'

As the trial neared its end, it was left to Jane's counsel, Mr Bevan, to argue for his client's life. Although he was unable to call any defence witnesses, in his closing speech, Bevan made valiant efforts on her behalf.

He first argued the identity of the dead baby, saying that nobody had proved beyond reasonable doubt that the baby was actually William Beard. He then proposed that Jane might have knelt down to drink while holding the baby, and he might have accidentally slipped from her arms into the water, causing Jane to panic and run away. Bevan insisted to the jury that the prosecution had not managed to demonstrate that Jane intended to drown the child, arguing that the witnesses who had allegedly heard Jane confessing to killing the baby might have misheard or just misinterpreted her words.

When the defence rested, Mr Justice Talfourd summed up the evidence for the jury, which, according to the contemporary newspapers, he did with great care and fairness. It then only remained for the jury to deliberate and return their verdict.

The jury found Jane Chenoweth 'Guilty' of the wilful murder of William Beard, although they made a strong recommendation for mercy on account of her age. Promising to forward their concerns to the proper authorities, Mr Justice Talfourd put on his black cap and, in a voice that frequently broke with barely-suppressed emotion, passed sentence of death on Jane Chenoweth.

On hearing his words, Jane began to cry hysterically, screaming that both John Pearce and Inspector Nash had been giving false testimony against her. Sobbing piteously, she clung desperately to the rail at the front of the dock and warders had to prise her fingers from it in order to remove her from the court.

Jane's youth, coupled with the fact that she had made determined efforts to have baby William taken into the Truro Union on the night before his murder, aroused some sympathy among the inhabitants of Cornwall, who organised several petitions for a reprieve. Missives were sent to the Secretary of State from a number of Cornish towns including Truro, Falmouth, Liskeard, Camborne, Redruth, Helston and Penzance.

The petitions, along with the jury's recommendation for mercy, proved successful and, in a letter from Under-Secretary Horatio Waddington, dated 6 August 1853, it was announced:

> Viscount Palmerston having carefully considered your Application on behalf of Jane Chenoweth, I have the satisfaction to acquaint you that under all the circumstances, he has felt warranted in advising her Majesty to commute the prisoner's sentence to transportation for life.

Note: The date of the murder of William Beard is variously given in the contemporary newspapers as 11, 12 and 14 June 1853.

12

'I NEVER TOUCHED IT'

Calstock, 1856

During the nineteenth century, many a child born at home was in grave danger of dying during or shortly after delivery. More often than not it was a genuine case of accidental death, but concealment of a baby's death by the mother was a crime. In such cases there was always the possibility that 'concealment' acted as a smokescreen for the far greater crime of infanticide. When an unmarried woman, or a woman whose husband had been absent for a long time, had given birth secretly and the newly-born infant died, the mother was rarely if ever convicted of infanticide, but many a case of concealment was tried by the courts. It was naturally impossible to establish whether the child had been deliberately killed or not, and there was also widespread recognition, even acceptance, of the fact that women in such cases normally lived in poverty and poor conditions, which mitigated if not fully excused the crime. One such instance occurred in Cornwall in 1856.

At about 9 p.m. on 23 March, Easter Sunday, Mary Ann Roberts, aged about twenty-three, and Mary Smitheran, both retired for the night at their house at Calstock. Two of the Roberts children were already sleeping in the same bed that the women regularly shared. Mary Ann Roberts' parents, Mr and Mrs Dordge, lived next door. Her husband had been absent for about three years, and several times recently a suspicious Mary had suggested that she must be in the family way, but Mary Ann always firmly denied it.

Between three and four o'clock in the morning, Mary Ann told her friend that she had to get up as her father had just called her. Mary told her it was still too early, and she had no intention of going to work until after she had had her breakfast. She asked Mary Ann the time, but the latter said she did not know as the clock had

Calstock, 1915. (Authors' collection)

stopped. Listening for a moment, Mary assured her she could hear it ticking. Mary Ann came back to bed again, and Mary went back to sleep.

About half an hour later Mary awoke and found her crying. She asked Mary Ann what the matter was, but the latter did not reply. On asking her again, Mary Ann said it was nothing. Mary listened and heard someone choking in the bed. Mary Ann was then in the bed, as were the two children. Mary said, 'Mrs Roberts, what is the matter, is Billy choking?'

She said he was only catching his breath, as he did from time to time. She got out of bed, and said Mary ought to go downstairs as well.

Mary Ann went downstairs where there was a light and a fire was burning in the grate, but Mary Smitheran could still hear the sound of a baby crying and choking. This went on for some time, until she began to get impatient and asked Mary Ann when she was coming back to bed.

By this stage, Mary Ann realised that it was impossible to hide the truth any longer. She came to the foot of the stairs, saying, 'I have got a child, and for God's sake don't never split.' After taking three steps upstairs, she slipped and fell over. Mary Smitheran went down to help her back on her feet. Meanwhile Mary Ann's mother, Mary Dordge, who lived next door and had been alarmed by the noise, came round to ask what the matter was. Mary Ann repeated her instruction to her friend to say nothing, after which she assured her mother that everything was all right.

Mary told Mary Ann a second time to come back to bed, and said they could get up and do any necessary work later. Instead Mary Ann said she could not come to bed, but picked up her clothes and went into her mother's house.

Next day Mary Ann Venning, who lived a couple of doors away in the same road, was spoken to and went into Mary Ann Roberts's house, where she saw a dead baby boy lying on the floor in front of the kitchen stove. Mrs Dordge was also there, and at her request she washed the tiny body, which was still quite warm. She noticed a small bruise on the front of the neck, and a little mark on the breast. As she carried the body upstairs she found Mary Ann Roberts in bed, complaining that she felt very unwell.

'Oh! Mrs Roberts,' exclaimed Mary Ann Venning, 'how came you to have a child like this?'

'I never did nothing to it,' was the reply. 'I never touched it.'

She put the child's body in the cradle, and the surgeon, Henry Turner Wood, was called. He briefly saw Mary Ann Roberts in the bedroom, and after making a few enquiries said he would return to carry out a post-mortem examination in two days' time with Mr Sleeman, another surgeon, and Constable Crocker.

On Wednesday, 26 March, Mary Ann Roberts's mother, Mary Dordge, brought in the body of the child, a fully-grown male infant, of average length and weight. The surgeons concluded that it had not been born prematurely. Its features were swollen and livid, particularly around the lips, and there were scratches and circular cuts on the chest, neck and face, and a bruise 3ins long on the front part of the neck. Wood examined the skin over the bruised surface in the neck, and found the parts beneath much congested and laden with blood. The lungs were somewhat congested and dark red, indicating that respiration had taken place. While the liver, abdomen and chest were healthy, the surface of the brain was much congested. In his opinion the cause of death was congestion of the brain, produced by deliberate pressure in front of the neck administered after the child's birth, in order to stop him from breathing.

This alone was enough to warrant the arrest of Mary Ann Roberts on a charge of murder, and she was taken into custody.

On 30 July she was tried at Bodmin Crown Court before Mr Baron Martin, charged with wilful murder and concealment of pregnancy; she pleaded 'Not Guilty'. The counsel for the prosecution were Mr Coleridge and Mr Buller, and Mr Carter for the defence. For the prosecution, Mr Coleridge stressed that the prisoner was a married woman. When the offence took place, her husband had been absent for about three years, so she had every reason for wishing to conceal her condition, and thus the presence of the infant, from her husband. Mrs Smitheran had long suspected the prisoner of being with child, and charged her with it more than once, although the prisoner had always stoutly denied it.

As witnesses, he called Mary Smitheran, Mary Ann Venning, and the surgeons Henry Turner Wood and Richard Sleeman. When Wood was cross-examined by the judge, he admitted it was possible that the pressure to the front of the neck might have been applied by the mother during the delivery, and the bruise might have been caused during self-delivery.

At this point the judge handed to the witness his deposition, in which he had stated that the bruise on part of the child's neck was in a place where it would probably occur in case of self-delivery. The witness confirmed that the deposition was correct.

For the defence, Mr Carter claimed that there was simply not enough evidence to convict her. As he was proceeding with his comments upon the case, the judge was looking over the written evidence. At length he stopped Mr Carter, and told the jury that he was sure it was quite insufficient to support a charge of murder. The entire case rested on mere doubt and suspicion.

Nobody was surprised when the jury gave a verdict of 'Not Guilty'. Mary Ann Roberts was no murderess, but whether she had deliberately meant to kill the child or whether it had been a tragic accident, nobody would know. She walked free from court.

13

'I HAVE BEEN DRIVEN TO IT'

Maker, 1856

In the summer of 1856 Sergeant-Major Benjamin Robinson was in charge of several prisoners on board the convict ship *Runnymede*. Lying in Plymouth Sound, the vessel was about to proceed to Swan River, western Australia, with some of the convicts. Among those serving under Robinson was forty-four-year-old Corporal William Nevan.

Some months previously, Nevan had been a private under Robinson's command at Dartmoor Prison. Unfailingly conscientious and strict towards those for whom he was responsible, Robinson found it necessary to speak to Nevan on several occasions for not attending to his arms and accoutrements, and for various trifling deficiencies in his duty. As a result, the latter harboured feelings of deep resentment against him, and was once heard to say that if the senior man found fault with him again, he would put a bullet in his musket and shoot him dead.

This grudge continued unabated after they had left Dartmoor and joined the ship. At the end of May, Nevan told his commanding officer, Major Russell, that Robinson was making life difficult for him. In particular, Robinson was often reversing or rescinding the orders Nevan gave to the other convicts, and he felt they had reached the point where they could no longer work together. Nevan asked if it would be possible to leave the ship, to which Russell answered that he was prepared to put him on shore, but if so he would have to leave the service, and would be unable to return to Dartmoor. In addition, any expenses incurred, and the cost of his outfit would be deducted from his pension, which he might lose altogether. This last possibility had previously been uttered by Robinson, and Nevan had thought it was no more than a threat. Now he realised it was a possibility, and faced with these bleak prospects, Nevan reluctantly agreed to stay where he was.

On the afternoon of 1 June, Robinson paraded the men as usual, and inspected Nevan as well as several other corporals, paying particular attention to their appearance and firelocks. After this inspection the rest of the men went below, but Nevan remained on deck with his musket. When Robinson inspected the men he found that one of the soldiers, Private Sullivan, was missing. He saw Nevan on deck and told him to fetch Sullivan – who was found cleaning his musket. Sullivan went up the starboard side to the sergeant major, and the latter began inspecting Sullivan's musket.

Seeing his chance, Nevan then went up the steps to the poop, faced Robinson, placed the gun against his hip and fired. The shot took off two of Robinson's fingers and then entered his abdomen. As he cried out and fell, a pensioner, Fenton Kinnaird, rushed at Nevan, who was walking casually down the steps, and seized Nevan by the collar.

'Do not have such a hold of me,' Nevan replied calmly. 'Loose your hold. I have done it, I have been driven to it.'

Later that afternoon he was taken into custody by Inspector Damerel from the police at Plymouth. He escorted Nevan to the room where Robinson was lying dead, and charged him with shooting him.

'If I did it, it was an accident,' Nevan said. 'I did not know it was my gun that went off; it caught in the coop and went off by accident; at times I am not all right; at certain times I do not know what I am about; he threatened to take away my pension.'

An inquest was held on board *Runnymede* on 2 June. The families of Robinson, a widow and four children, and of Nevan, a wife and five children, were present, many of them crying loudly much of the time. A verdict of wilful murder was returned by the jury, and Nevan was committed to Bodmin Gaol. The press commented that the authorities were partly to blame by sending out convicts with a guard of thirty soldiers and no commissioned officer in command. Had an officer been there, it was believed, better discipline would have been observed, and the crime would probably not have been committed.

Nevan was tried at Bodmin Crown Court before Mr Baron Martin on 30 July, and pleaded 'Not Guilty'. Robert Collier and Mr Holdsworth were the counsel for the prosecution, and Mr Coleridge for the defence. After outlining the facts of the case, Collier called several members of the convict guard as witnesses. As Sullivan gave his evidence, Nevan sat down and leaned forward with his face in his hands.

Coleridge then addressed the jury on behalf of Nevan, arguing that the gun had gone off accidentally. The prisoner, he said, was telling the truth when he said it had become caught in the hen coop. The gun was loaded and capped in the ordinary course of his duty, and it could not be proved that he had aimed deliberately at Robinson. No witnesses could be found to confirm the exact position of the prisoner when the weapon was fired. Moreover, as the sentry and Sullivan were standing close to Robinson at the time, Nevan was not likely to have discharged his musket intentionally and risked shooting the other men; and, in his view, he was unlikely to have committed such a deed intentionally at three o'clock in the afternoon.

Robert Collier, later Baron Monkswell.
(Collier family collection)

There was no proof of motive for such a crime, Coleridge continued, and it could not be assumed that the prisoner would have murdered Robinson merely because he had taken a dislike to him. He then tried to discredit Kinnaird's statement regarding threats used by Nevan towards Robinson, and as to the expression Kinnaird said the prisoner made use of when he seized him by the collar after the discharge of the musket. He was confident that the jury would press for a verdict of acquittal.

'Till I hear your verdict,' he said, 'I shall take the liberty of thinking there is such doubt, and, if there be that doubt, leave him to the judgment of a Higher Power. If you have any doubt, leave him his life, and if he is innocent he has a right to it, and which will be a sore burden, too heavy to bear, if he is not.'

As the judge summed up the evidence, he remarked that, with regard to the alleged absence of motive, it was well known that every year persons were found to take the lives of others for reasons that appeared wholly inadequate to people in general. He also commented on statements made by the prisoner to Kinnaird and to Police Inspector Damerel, told the jury that they must form their own opinion, and had to do their duty both towards the prisoner and the public.

The jury retired for ten minutes and returned with a verdict of 'Guilty'. When Nevan was asked by the clerk of arraigns whether he wished to say anything, he remained silent. As the judge donned the black cap to pass sentence, he told Nevan that, during the trial, everything that could possibly be used in his defence had been done by the learned counsel who had defended him. He himself entirely concurred with the verdict of 'Guilty', and he did not see how any other verdict could have been returned on the evidence. A petition, presumably from the people of his hometown, had been placed in his hands, and he would forward it to the Secretary of State, but he advised the prisoner not to raise his hopes.

Nevertheless, the judge seemed quite emotional as he passed the death sentence, while Nevan himself exclaimed, 'The Lord look upon me.' About three days after being condemned, he admitted that the shooting had been no accident, but he had been driven to it by anger at Robinson's 'harshness'.

Over his last few days he was attended to by the Revd J.R. Shortland, the Roman Catholic priest of the Cornwall Mission at Bodmin. He spent much of his time in reading and prayer, and had evidently given up any hope of a reprieve. Later that week he had a final meeting with his wife; he told her to bring their children up in the Catholic faith, and tell them that 'they should never allow their evil passions to overcome them'. While he acknowledged to the priest the justness of his sentence, he said he had led a religious life until the last three years, and had then fallen away through inattention to religious duties. Now he was fully prepared, he would die happy.

On the morning of 11 August, the Roman Catholic ceremony of Extreme Unction was administered to him in the cell by the priest. A crowd of about 3,000 came to watch the execution. Before leaving the cell, he exclaimed, 'This is the day of battle; Satan has been tempting me, but I will resist him.' To the assembled crowds, he admitted the justness of his sentence, claiming he was willing to die for it, 'and may the Lord have mercy on my soul.' Three minutes before he shot Robinson, he went on, 'it came into my mind to shoot him; I turned round and saw him smile, and then I thought I must shoot him.'

After the hangman William Calcraft had done his work, the streets of Bodmin were packed. Several enterprising stallholders were doing good business, and the town,

it was noticed with asperity by one newspaper reporter, 'presented all the appearance of a fair day'. Nevertheless, others showed some finer feelings in subscribing £15 for the relief of Mrs Nevan and their children.

Old place of execution, Bodmin Gaol. (Authors' collection)

14

'A VERY FORLORN, NEGLECTED OUTCAST'

St Stephen-by-Launceston, 1862

During the summer of 1862 John Doidge, a labourer of about thirty who lodged at St Stephen-by-Launceston, found work hard to come by, and, with no money coming in, he was starving. His landlord, Mr Sutton, had ceased giving him food, and was threatening to turn him out on the street. The house in which he was lodging was opposite that of fifty-seven-year-old Roger Drew. A widower who had previously lived in Gosport, Drew's late wife had been in service, and he now lived alone, trading as a grocer and carpenter. It was commonly supposed that he kept a large amount of money in his house.

Drew and Doidge both frequented the same public house, the Smith's Arms, and on the evening of 7 June 1862 they were seen at the inn having a friendly conversation together.

Early next morning Mary Martin went to buy something from Drew's shop, finding the shutter had not been put up and the door was locked. Looking through the window, she saw Drew lying face-down on the floor in a pool of blood. The tables and chairs had been scattered about, suggesting that the premises had been burgled. At once she went to the Smith's Arms to tell Mr Bassett, the landlord, and Mr Cory, a friend who was there, of what she had seen. Cory immediately went to Drew's house to see the sorry business for himself. He knocked at the door, then looked in and saw the dead man lying in a pool of blood.

The police were contacted at once. As they arrived, Mrs Sutton, Doidge's landlady, noticed Doidge trying to conceal a large billhook, which he used for cutting wood, behind a water barrel. Enquiries by the police led them to the meeting both men had had in the inn, and Inspector Woods took Doidge into custody. Mr and Mrs Sutton told him that Doidge had not arrived back at his lodgings until between 3 and 4 a.m., and had unusually been up by 6 a.m. washing his clothes and boots. When the clothes were examined blood was found on his coat, shirt and trousers. He was charged with the murder, but protested his innocence. Taken into custody and handcuffed, he went to the lock-up at Egloskerry, two miles away.

When Drew's house was examined by police, it was found that a cash box in his bedroom had been broken into. There were bloodstains on the stairs and in the bedroom, and it was thought that Drew had been attacked while getting ready for bed that night, as he had a slipper on one foot and an unlaced boot on the other. A post-mortem that afternoon, conducted by Dr Thompson and Dr Felce, found that the blow on his head was so severe that death must have been instantaneous.

It was apparent that Doidge's life had not been a happy one. The press called him 'a very forlorn, neglected outcast'; born the illegitimate son of 'a most sinful mother', he was committed at the age of three months to an elderly foster mother who took little interest in him during childhood. At the age of nine he had been sent to work in a farmhouse and soon fell into a life of petty thieving.

Some six years later he took a rather better farm servant's job with Mr Yeo of Launceston. While in his employ he stole from the children's moneyboxes and burgled a house – the residence of Mr Kenner – in the same parish. When Yeo casually mentioned the matter to him the next day, commenting particularly on the theft on moneyboxes from which several sovereigns had been stolen, Doidge said it was a lie. He asserted that Kenner had not lost any sovereigns, only sixpenny and fourpenny pieces. It was a clumsy remark which more or less amounted to a confession. After that he had nothing to lose by admitting he was the guilty party, and he offered to show Yeo the money, which he had hidden under a tree. He was taken into custody, and although aged only fifteen, he was sentenced to nine months' imprisonment with hard labour.

It was not the only evidence of a rebellious streak, or perhaps more accurately a criminal mind. Two years before this theft, he had been suspected of setting fire to a house in the village.

However, these misdemeanours paled into insignificance alongside the apparent taking of another man's life. From the moment of his arrest he made no effort to deny having killed Drew. He gave no signs that it weighed heavily on his conscience, and during the next few weeks he ate, drank and slept as usual, seemingly unaffected by the fate hanging over him.

He was charged at Bodmin Assizes, appearing before Mr Justice Williams in a trial lasting two days, on 6 and 7 August, at the end of which he was found guilty. Afterwards he confessed to the chaplain that he had entered Drew's house only intending to rob him, and was then 'urged on to murder'. Though he had never married, he admitted to having fathered a child, and it was after difficulties between him and the mother of this infant that he had enlisted in the Royal Marines for a time.

Bodmin Gaol. (Authors' collection)

On the morning of 18 August, a woman called at the gaol. She insisted that she was Mrs Doidge, and asked to see her husband. As she could not produce a marriage certificate or any other proof, the governor did not believe her and refused to grant her request. Determined not to be thwarted, she declared that she had married him eight years previously, and had been living at Liskeard ever since, but it was to no avail.

Two other women came and presented themselves. They claimed that they were suffering from sore necks, and they begged the governor to let the convict's hand touch them after he had been hanged, as they were sure it would cure them. Like the visitor who called herself Mrs Doidge, they also went away with their request unsatisfied.

At around noon the same day he was hanged by William Calcraft. Those who used to complain habitually about the gross spectacle of public executions would doubtless have been glad to know that Doidge was destined to be the last person hanged in public in Cornwall. The next person in the county to share the same fate, Selina Wadge, convicted in 1878 of murdering her son, was executed privately inside the gaol.

Note: For the case of Selina Wadge, see *Cornish Murders*.

15

'IF IT IS DONE, IT IS DONE'

In 1864, John Stickland married Mrs Wilmot Miles, a widow with two young children. Mrs Miles' first husband, Thomas, had left her financially comfortable on his death, her inheritance including both money and property in California. Yet it seemed as though Stickland married for love, rather than money, as he and Wilmot lived happily together at Stickland's home in Angarrack. Stickland, who was employed at Hayle foundry as a boiler maker by Messrs Harvey & Co., and also kept a small farm, had no objection to his step-children, Elizabeth and Thomas, living with him and even allowed his mother-in-law to move into an annexe of his home. (The relationship between Stickland and Wilmot's mother was a complex one since, as well as being his mother-in-law, Grace Stickland, was also John's aunt.)

In 1865, Wilmot gave birth to a daughter, Maria Bowden Stickland, who instantly became the apple of her father's eye. However, soon after her birth, both of Maria's parents became ill. Her father suffered from frequent nose bleeds and disorders of his stomach and liver, which sent him into a state of depression, while Mrs Stickland became consumptive, her health declining steadily until she eventually died from her illness on 1 May 1868.

John Stickland was distraught at losing his beloved wife, even more so when he found that he did not even have sufficient money to bury her. Mrs Stickland's inheritance had meant that the couple had never had any financial concerns and had always spent money freely and extravagantly, living a rather lavish lifestyle. When his wife died, John quickly discovered that, under the terms of her will, all the money she had inherited from Thomas Miles went to Elizabeth and Thomas junior, the children of her first marriage and, with his mother-in-law on hand to make sure that her daughter's wishes were carried out, John and Maria were left without a penny to their names.

On 3 May, with Wilmot Stickland still lying in her coffin in the house, neighbour Edward Stephens called to pay his respects and see how John was bearing up.

When Stephens asked John how he was, he replied sorrowfully, 'I am very bad. My poor wife is dead and I have no money to bury her. My friends have all left me and I'm a man ruined forever.'

The neighbour tried to cheer him up, telling him, 'John, you have plenty of money somewhere.'

'I cannot find any,' replied Strickland dolefully.

'Where is your bank book?'

'I cannot find it,' said Stickland.

'Then you have plenty of things that you can convert to money. Where is your gold watch?' asked Stephens.

'Gone,' said Strickland.

'Then where is your gold stick?'

'I cannot find it.'

'What about the deeds to your house?'

Angarrack. (© N. Sly)

'They have disappeared,' Stickland said, telling his visitor that he sincerely believed his late wife's family and the Miles family together were conspiring against him, taking what should rightly come to him and his daughter, and that his wife's mother was 'as bad a rogue as any'.

Stephens asked if Wilmot had made a will, telling John that Maria would surely have part of it.

'There is nothing left for Maria but a debt of £60 and I shall never be able to pay it,' John told Stephens, who then said that he should call all of his friends together and ask for their assistance.

'My friends have all deserted me. They will not come near me,' answered Stickland.

The neighbour suggested that Stickland should go and see the vicar, who was a 'real gentleman' and would be able to speak plainly to him and advise him how to bury his wife but Stickland, who was normally a very private person, baulked at the idea. He seemed very confused, telling his neighbour, 'I cannot speak. I don't know what is the matter with me. I don't know what voice I am in. I can't tell what anyone is saying two minutes together.'

Stephens advised him to sell something from the house and use the money to pay for Wilmot's funeral.

'If I do that, I shall be put in prison, as nothing in this house is mine.'

Stephens eventually left, having grave concerns for John Stickland's well-being and fearing that he might hang himself. Stickland had a family history of mental illness; his uncle had died in an asylum and his grandmother was described as 'deranged', although she was said to be 'easy mad, not wicked mad'. Stephens promised to do whatever he could to help and, later that afternoon, went back to see John to tell him that he had found someone who was willing to buy his cow. By that time, John had sunk even further into depression and appeared not to understand what Stephens was saying. His neighbours tried everything they could to lift his melancholy mood, one of them telling him, 'Cheer up. I have buried two wives and you see I am getting on very well.' Yet, in spite of his neighbours' efforts, John seemed inconsolable.

On the night of Sunday 3 May, he went to bed early, taking little Maria into his bedroom, where she had slept since the death of her mother. Later that night, eighteen-year-old Matilda Gilbert, the family servant, locked up the house and retired to her own bed. The night passed peacefully and, when Matilda got up at seven o'clock the next morning, everything was exactly as she had left it the night before.

There was, however, no sign of John Stickland and his daughter. At nine o'clock, Grace Stickland interrupted Matilda's morning chores to ask her the whereabouts of some black material, as she wanted to prepare mourning clothes for her two grandchildren. Matilda knew that there was some black cloth in John Stickland's bedroom and sent eight-year-old Elizabeth Miles in to fetch it. Moments later, Elizabeth ran back into the kitchen to say that John lay dead in his bed, with a knife on the pillow.

In a state of panic, Matilda called for a neighbour, John Burnett, who rushed into Stickland's room and was met by a terrible spectacle.

Little Maria lay on the blood-soaked bed, her throat cut so deeply that her head was almost severed from her body. Close by lay John Stickland, an open razor on his pillow, bleeding heavily from a deep wound in his throat and obviously very near death. 'What have you done, John?' Burnett asked him, but Stickland was unable to speak and, although his lips moved, no words came out.

Surgeon James Mudge was sent for and, while he could do nothing for Maria, Mudge was able to stitch and bandage the wound in her father's throat, although the injury was so severe that Mudge held out little hope for his survival. Stickland, meanwhile, fought desperately to die. Throughout that day and the next, he made repeated desperate attempts to tear off his bandages and reopen the wound. Told that Maria had died, Stickland wailed, 'Lord have mercy, what have I done?' From that moment on, his only comment on his daughter's death was a sorrowful 'If it is done, it is done.'

An inquest held by coroner John Roscorla returned a verdict of 'wilful murder' against John Stickland. Against all the odds, he survived his attempted suicide and found himself on trial, appearing before Mr Baron Channell at Bodmin Assizes.

Asked if he pleaded 'Guilty' or 'Not Guilty' to the charge of wilful murder against him, Stickland appeared confused. 'I do not know, sir,' he replied, at which Channell recorded a plea of 'Not Guilty' and the trial began.

Assisted by Mr Pendarves, Mr Lopes, for the prosecution, outlined the events of 3 and 4 May for the jury, having first told them that it would be their painful task to decide whether Stickland was to live or whether, by his own act, he had forfeited his life to the offended laws of the country. It was the jury's job, said Lopes, to put aside any natural feelings of pity that they might have for the defendant and discharge their duty to society. Lopes continued to say that he expected the argument for the defence would be that, at the time of the murder of his daughter, John Stickland was insane. The counsel for the prosecution reminded the jury that, in the eyes of the law, a man was assumed sane at the time of his crime unless proven otherwise and that, although the accused was undoubtedly in a low state when Maria was murdered, his depression didn't equate to insanity.

The prosecution then went on to call Matilda Gilbert, who was followed into the witness box by Grace Stickland, Elizabeth Miles (the mother of Wilmot's first husband), PC James Gigg and several neighbours of John Stickland, including John Burnett and Edward Stephens. Even little Elizabeth Miles testified, tearfully telling the court about finding the body of her stepsister and her injured stepfather on the morning of 4 May.

Surgeon Mr Mudge had been the Sticklands' regular doctor, as well as having been called to the scene of the murder, conducting a post-mortem examination on Maria and subsequently treating John Stickland's injuries. There were three incisions on Stickland's throat, the deepest of which had severed one of his main arteries. Mudge had taken possession of a bloody razor from his bedroom, which he then handed to PC James Gigg.

Tellingly, Mudge revealed that, at the time of the murder, Stickland sported a long beard, suggesting that he did not use a razor regularly and would not have had one to hand. The surgeon had to cut off the patient's beard to allow him to inspect the damage to his throat.

Speaking of Stickland's mental state, Mudge told the court that he was naturally a rather melancholy man, with a 'low and despondent disposition', which Mudge attributed to his stomach and liver problems. Yet, at all times, Stickland had seemed rational. The only explanation that Mudge could offer for Stickland's crime was that the death of his wife, his own health problems, and the discovery that he had absolutely no money, might have made him particularly prone to committing rash acts.

As expected, defence counsel Mr Folkard's contention was that his client was insane at the time of the murder and simply did not appreciate that what he was doing was wrong. The jury obviously agreed with this explanation, since they acquitted forty-year-old John Stickland of the wilful murder of his daughter on the grounds of insanity, after only a brief deliberation, leaving the judge to sentence him to be detained during Her Majesty's pleasure. It was revealed at the trial that, when Stickland's house was searched immediately after the murder, no money and not a morsel of food had been found.

Note: John Burnett is alternatively named John Barnett in some contemporary accounts of the murder.

16

'I DON'T REMEMBER ANYTHING ABOUT IT'

Chacewater, 1874

Emily Mitchell was born near Perranwell around 1846. She was barely a grown woman when she married Thomas Richards, but their life together was destined to be a short one. In 1867 he left her and their young child to fend for themselves, while he emigrated to the United States of America with vague, meaningless assurances about returning to them once he had made his fortune. At first he was conscientious enough to send Emily money at regular intervals, but soon this arrangement stopped. To support herself she went into service, leaving her child in the care of her mother and father, and in 1872 she took up a position working for Mr Furneaux, a grocer at Penryn.

In June 1874 she left her employer and returned to her parents, who lived near Perranwell. This arrangement did not last long, and she evidently wanted to be more independent. On 23 July her mother accompanied her to Penzance, where she made some enquiries about accommodation and then took lodgings in Adelaide Street, the home of Miss Louisa Keate, under the name of Mrs Rapson. What had become of her child by this time is unknown, and one can only assume that he or she must have died young. However, there was another on the way, for at the time she was about four months pregnant. A few weeks later her mother came to visit her and brought her £10.

On 22 November, she gave birth to a baby boy and registered his birth on 9 December, giving his name as Samuel Rapson. The next day, wearing a black dress with a black and red check shawl, she told Miss Keate that she was leaving, and planned to go first to Truro, and then back to her home, which was 'near

Plymouth'. Miss Keate's sister, Caroline Kent, offered to accompany her as she took the child and various possessions, including a box, a black bag, a parcel and a lamp. She apparently had no home near Plymouth, and this was only the first of several contradictory statements, a number of which were proved to be untrue. Was she already trying to lay a false trail in an attempt to throw any witnesses off the scent, should she later be arrested for doing something very wrong?

The two women went to Redruth station. From there, Emily Richards and her baby son went on to Truro, where she hired a cab and was driven to Chacewater. At Chacewater railway station she found a railway connection to Perranwell, four miles south-east, very close to her parents' home at Carnon Downs. She took a box of possessions to the parcels office and asked for it to be sent to Perranwell, where she said she would collect it later, then waited for another cab and asked the driver to take her and Samuel back towards Chacewater. After they had gone about four miles, she asked the cabman if he would turn down a road which would take her directly to her father's house, another four miles away. A few hundred yards further on, she asked him to drop them off, and paid the fare. He lit the lamp for her and watched as mother and child went off into the night.

Not long afterwards she met fifteen-year-old Charlotte Harvey, who was accompanied by her younger sister. Emily asked the girl the way to Baldhu, and also to Wheal Faithey pump. The road they were on would have led her in a straight line to her father's house, but to go to Baldhu – which was in another direction entirely – would have meant walking almost twice the distance. Wheal Faithey pump, about 140 yards off the main road, had been the shaft of a working mine which had now fallen into disuse. It was about 18 fathoms deep, the shaft was partly covered over by planking, and a windlass and bucket were placed over it so people could draw water. Charlotte and her sister led Emily towards the pump, and as they made their way Samuel started crying. The girls asked if they could see the baby, but Emily would not let them, saying that it was wrapped up to keep it warm and she did not wish to disturb it. As soon as the pump came into sight she thanked them and asked them to leave her.

Chacewater. (© N. Sly)

A little later that evening she called at the house of John and Grace Stephens, who lived about 150 yards from the pump, to ask the way to Baldhu and Carnon. Grace was at home, and though she did not know Emily, she had sympathy for this young woman trying to find her way around the countryside on a dark wet December night, with little more than an umbrella for protection against the elements and only a lamp to show her where she was going.

A few minutes later John came in. Grace had offered to go outside and show Emily the way, but John offered to walk a little further with her and ensure she was taking the right direction to Carnon. On a night like that, in the middle of nowhere, it would be too easy for somebody unfamiliar with the area to make a mistake. When he asked her for her name, she told him, adding that she was the daughter of John Mitchell, and was going home to him. As John Stephens took her back to the main road, he noticed that in addition to an umbrella and a lamp, she was also carrying a bag.

When he returned to the farmhouse and discussed it with Grace, both of them thought there was something not quite right. If the young woman knew where her father's house was, why was she asking the way? Was she ill or confused, or could she be an impostor merely pretending to be Mr Mitchell's daughter? He went out again to see if the woman was still around. She had not gone far and he overtook her at the bottom of the garden. She asked him the way to Crosslanes, and he gave her further directions. It struck him that she seemed very nervous, and gave the impression that she did not really know where she wanted to go.

Between nine and ten o'clock that night, after a long journey on foot, she arrived at her parents' house. When they greeted her, she explained that she had lost her way, and a woman (presumably Charlotte Harvey) with a child had 'put her right'.

After staying there for about three days she suddenly disappeared, without leaving any clue as to where she was going. On the evening of the day that she left, a miner passed the well and noticed a piece of flannel lying on the edge of the well. He took it home and tried to find an owner for it. When Emily had lodged in Penzance, her landlady had noticed some flannel in her possession that was sewn in a particular way – the flannel found at the well was sewn in the same style.

On 14 December Constable Allen was alerted to the fact that a suspicious-looking woman with a child had been seen in Chacewater, and as it was feared that something might have happened to the child, he realised enquiries had to be made. He ordered a thorough search of the well on 15 December. Nothing was found at first, but they decided to try again on New Year's Eve. This time a miner was let down into the well, and about 4 fathoms from the shaft he found a bag floating on the water. Inside was the body of a male child.

The body was examined, but as neither the landlady at Penzance nor her sister saw it, no identification could be made. The medical evidence found no marks of violence; death could have been caused by asphyxia. Symptoms were consistent with death by drowning, but the medical man would not say they were inconsistent with asphyxia from other causes. Judging by the state of the body and the general circumstances, he believed that the child had been drowned.

An inquest was held at the Red Lion Inn in Chacewater, by John Carlyon, the county coroner, on 5 January 1875. Constable Allen commented that he had been prompted by rumours of the disappearance of a child to make enquiries, and in this had been helped by Superintendent Marshall of Truro and Sergeant Brooks of St Agnes. John Stephens mentioned that sometime after seven o'clock on the evening of 10 December he had seen a light near the pump, and thought somebody must have gone there for water. He then described the visit that John Mitchell's daughter had paid him and his wife, emphasising that he was reasonably sure she did not have a child with her.

Also present at the inquest was her mother, Mary Ann Mitchell. She confirmed that her daughter had married Thomas Richards, and had been at home ever since his departure for America. No further evidence was offered, and although the evidence was largely circumstantial, the jury returned a verdict of wilful murder against Emily Richards.

A major search was now mounted for her. As *Freeman's Journal & Daily Commercial Advertiser* wrote in February 1875 when reporting the next stage of events, if she was eventually brought to trial for the murder of her child, 'her discovery will form a romantic episode worthy of our most imaginative novelists.'

What happened next was later pieced together by Colonel Gilbert, Chief County Constable. On 4 February 1875 he was given information about a young woman from Cornwall believed to be Emily Richards, who had crossed from Plymouth to Cherbourg in a Hamburg-American steamer on 19 December last. While she was travelling by rail between Cherbourg and Paris in January she was apparently attacked, robbed, and left unconscious. A guard found her when the train arrived at Nantes, and she was taken to hospital. A few days later she regained consciousness and, when questioned, gave her name and said she had come to France from Plymouth. Accommodation was found for her in a mission home in Paris, managed by a Miss Lee, and shortly afterwards she went to live as a servant with a Miss Gray, matron of the Young Women's Christian Association at 88 Faubourg St Honoré. Meanwhile the British Ambassador in France, Lord Lyons, forwarded all this information to London.

Colonel Gilbert then sent Superintendent Marshall to France so he could track the young woman down. He was given the necessary extradition papers for her and, with the help of a French detective, on 6 February he tracked her down in Paris. A gendarme accompanied him as he knocked on the door of the house. When a young woman answered the door, he immediately recognised her from the photograph he had been provided.

'Oh, Emily, I want you,' he said to her.

She hung her head in shame, and turned to walk away. Marshall told his French colleague that this was the person he was seeking, and the other man went to fetch her while Marshall explained the situation to Miss Gray. Emily was led back to Marshall, and as she looked at him, she said helplessly, 'Lord have mercy on me.'

Finding the wanted woman was one thing, but getting her back to Cornwall proved to be quite another. She was held in custody awaiting completion of the extradition, which was theoretically granted on 18 February. Marshall regularly asked the prefect when she would be handed over, but each time he was told that certain formalities had to be observed, and he must wait. These may have been connected with the fact that she apparently made no confession to anybody about having killed her son.

After what must have seemed an interminable wait to Marshall, she was handed over to him on the afternoon of 2 March. They crossed the Channel later that day, arrived at London by train at seven o'clock the next morning, left Paddington at nine o'clock by another train and reached Plymouth at about 5.20 p.m. for a 6.10 connection to Truro. At this final destination a crowd had gathered to see her, and she was taken to the police station. Among those who had come to watch were the inevitable press representatives, who had been following developments with interest. They remarked that she looked careworn, her voice was very hoarse when she spoke, and she was 'said to wander in her mind'.

Next day she was brought before the magistrates at Truro Town Hall and formally remanded. Before the evidence was heard, she was asked if she wanted a lawyer to appear on her behalf. 'I don't want anyone,' she answered weakly. 'What for?'

When told she was being remanded, she started to cry, saying, 'I don't remember anything about it.' Once she was questioned by the police, she seemed very vague about her movements during the previous few weeks. The only thing about which she was adamant was that she had been given £10 the previous year by her 'young man in America'. This was presumably Thomas Richards, assuming he had started sending her money again on an occasional or irregular basis. Perhaps she still expected him to return to England one day. Alternatively, she might have been referring to the shadowy Mr Rapson. If Mr Richards was still alive, and no divorce had taken place, any subsequent marriage would have been bigamous. Her remarks could, equally, have been a reflection of her confused state of mind.

At the hearing on 8 March before the Truro magistrates and the chairman, Revd T. Phillpotts, it was reported that while waiting for her case to be heard, she was in a 'semi-stupefied state' in the arms of a female attendant, and occasionally laughing. Her demeanour appeared very strange when she entered the court; she refused to enter the prisoners' dock, and laughed again when it appeared that nobody was going to force her to do so.

Among the witnesses called was Louisa Keate of Penzance, who had seen Emily when she took lodgings in July 1874. She was with her when the child, a healthy baby, was born. Caroline Kent (Louisa's sister) also appeared, saying that nobody had ever come to visit their guest (who had given her name as Mrs Rapson) except a woman whom she called her aunt, Mrs Francis, who gave her £10. 'Mrs Francis' was in court, but was not an aunt; she was in fact her mother.

Three others all testified to having seen the woman and her small child on 10 December. One was Alfred Elliott, the parcels porter; another was Samuel Buckingham, the platform policeman, both of whom had been on duty at Truro station that day. The third was Robert Youlden, the cab driver who had taken mother and baby son from Truro station to the top of Chacewater Hill, and had charged her 6s for the journey.

John and Grace Stephens both described their brief encounter with her. They were followed by Emily's mother, Mary Ann Mitchell, who confirmed that her daughter had come home after leaving Penryn and had given her money.

The appearance of each of these people in the witness box seemed to have no effect on Emily, but when her father John Mitchell stepped forward, she called out to him and burst into tears. At this her mother also broke down and cried. The chairman gave them a few moments to regain their composure before proceeding, then John Mitchell corroborated his wife's evidence.

Only two more witnesses had yet to be called. The first was William Hugo, the Chacewater surgeon, who had conducted a post-mortem examination on New Year's Day. He said that the child had been dead for between two and three weeks, the most likely cause of death being drowning. He had lived for more than a week, but Hugo could not put the age any more accurately than sometime between a fortnight and a month. He had found no signs of external violence. Finally, Edward Marshall was called to give confirmation that the prisoner in the dock was the same young woman whose photograph he had been given in order to find her in Paris.

There was speculation that the case might never reach trial if it could be proved or argued that she was insane. However, her solicitor contended that she might have accidentally stifled the child, in which case it would certainly not have been murder.

She went on trial for murder at Bodmin Assizes before Mr Justice Lush on 22 March. Mr Charles and Mr W. St Aubyn appeared for the prosecution, and Mr Collins for the defence. For most of the proceedings, Emily leant in the dock with her head on her hand, her eyes shut, as if half asleep.

There were no new witnesses, with Caroline Kent, Mr and Mrs Stephens, and Mary Ann Mitchell all called to repeat the evidence they had given at the previous hearing a fortnight earlier. Once again, the only time that Emily really seemed affected was when her father entered the witness box shortly after her mother, and Emily burst into tears. She tried to attract his attention, but he looked firmly ahead and refused to be distracted. After he had been called formally, the court asked him to stand down without putting any further questions to him. It was almost as if there was a feeling that to ask him anything would only prolong the agony for his daughter.

None of the basic facts, particularly the finding of the dead baby in the well, were disputed. Nevertheless, Collins argued that finding some flannel at the well did not constitute proof that the child was Emily's. The defence relied on the absence of any positive evidence from anybody who saw the prisoner kill her child.

In his summing up, the judge emphasised that in his view the circumstantial evidence was as strong as it could be. One witness might be mistaken, but surely a dozen could not be wrong. He told the jury that there was a difference between direct evidence and a chain of circumstantial evidence, and of the superior value in some instances of the latter. Each link on the chain of circumstantial evidence, he said, bore on the charge against the prisoner.

After retiring for about half an hour the jury returned a verdict of 'Not Guilty'. Throughout the trial Emily Richards had appeared to take little interest, but when the verdict was read out she fell back in a dead faint, and the judge declared that 'she must be discharged'.

With hindsight, the verdict must be that she was probably suffering from post-natal depression, and, in addition to this, she was either very simple-minded or slightly insane. The least charitable theory, but one which cannot be ruled out, is that she was an extremely clever actress who worked hard at weaving a web of deceit in order to cover up a cold-blooded murder. There are no records of what became of her after she left court, but she was fortunate to escape detention at Her Majesty's pleasure, the most common fate at that time for mothers who had killed their young offspring. It was likely that she had ended the life of her young son, and the fact that he met his death by drowning suggested a degree of deliberation, rather than accident. Yet as the evidence was purely circumstantial, she was lucky that nobody was ever able to prove beyond doubt that she was responsible for his death.

17

'WHATEVER IS DONE, I DID IT'

Helston, 1886

The expansion of the railway network in Cornwall, as throughout much of the country, provided increasing employment opportunities in the late-nineteenth century. One such navvy was Charles Shearman, who worked on the railway line being built between Helston and Gwinearv Road. On Saturday 17 July he was one of eight men paid off from the Helston railway works. He had an argument with his landlady, doubtless relating to his inability – or refusal – to settle his bills, left his lodgings, and went to Sithney to do the rounds of the village inns with his workmates, where he talked about going to look for further work at Camborne, seven miles away.

An agreeable time was evidently had by all, and by the end of the next day he was in no fit state to go anywhere. His friends left him sleeping it off in a sheltered spot by the roadside. When he came round he made his way a short distance to a farm at Great Wheal Vor, near Breage, where he laid down beside a haystack, covered himself with hay and went to sleep. The farm belonged to Thomas Polglaze, a forty-nine-year-old bachelor who lived with his spinster sister Rosina. Polglaze worked in the mines near Camborne, and got up early each Monday morning to work down the mine, spending the week in lodgings and returning home on Friday, where he would help his sister on the farm.

On Monday 19 July he got up about 3.30 a.m. for breakfast, his sister having got up before him. About half an hour later he had a look round the premises before setting out on his journey, and went to the rick, about thirty yards from the cottage. He came back soon afterwards and told Rosina that there was a strange person lying down in the hay. He asked her to accompany him to the farm, but she refused, fearing that if the person was a man, and if they surprised him suddenly, he could turn violent.

He then took out of the cupboard a large axe used for cutting turf, and went out with it. His sister said he looked very frightened. About ten minutes later he returned, bringing the axe with him, and told his sister he was going to fetch a policeman. He then left, and his frightened sister went to the neighbour for help. Shearman was then found to be the man lying in the hay; he was dead, with severe injuries to his head and face.

Helston, 1955. (Authors' collection)

Great Wheal Vor, 1857. (Authors' collection)

Polglaze went straight to Porthleven, about three miles away, to call a policeman, found Constable John Gill, and told him what he had done. He said he wished Gill to return with him at once as he had found a man lying in his hayrick. He related how he had spoken to the man three times and told him to move out as he had no right to be there. Receiving no reply, he had returned with an axe. The man had moved his shoulders and opened his eyes, but as he did not get up or speak, Polglaze had given him a blow over the head with the axe. Polglaze concluded by saying he did not know, but he was afraid, that the man was dead.

The policeman returned with Polglaze to the spot where the man was lying; they found that a crowd had gathered, after the cries of his sister had attracted attention. Shearman's body was covered with hay, but the right hand, arm, and hat were visible. Polglaze went into the house with the policeman and took the axe out of the cupboard, telling him it was the one with which he had done it.

'Whatever is done, I did it,' he admitted candidly to the crowd. When one of them asked why, he replied that he was afraid the man had firearms and would kill him. He was then taken into custody at Helston, and on Monday afternoon he appeared before the magistrates.

Enquiries revealed that after leaving his companions the previous evening Shearman had called at the village inn, but the landlord had refused to serve him as he had clearly had enough to drink already.

An inquest was held on 20 July in the schoolroom at Great Wheal Vor before Mr J.P. Grenfell, the county coroner. Polglaze told the jury that he had attacked the man 'through fear', and he thought the intruder had 'meant mischief'. The other witnesses at the inquest included Rosina Polglaze, Constable John Gill and his wife Emily, and Charles Keast, a miner who worked at Wheal Vor Mine, who had known Polglaze for about thirty years. Also, there was Charles Shearman's brother William, a dock labourer from Falmouth, who said he had not seen his brother for twenty years and thus could not positively identify him – but thought it probably was his brother.

A surgeon from Helston, Charles Bullmore, had conducted the post-mortem. On examining the head he found extensive fractures running across from the front to the back on the right side, the bones being broken in pieces and driven into the brain, and there were signs of haemorrhage in both ears. On removing the scalp he found bones on the right side of the head, the right side of the face, and the lower jaw, broken in pieces, and the brain very much injured. The base of the skull was dreadfully fractured. He examined the other organs of the body and found them perfectly healthy. A very hard blow with the peat axe would certainly have produced the injuries he had described, and it was clear that they had been the cause of Shearman's death. When asked by the foreman of the jury whether one blow would have caused the injuries, he said it would have to have been a very violent blow.

When the coroner asked Polglaze whether he wanted to ask Bullmore any questions, he said he did not, adding, 'I only gave him one blow on the head.' Polglaze was then invited to make any statement he wanted to, on oath. He described finding

Shearman on his property, and telling him to leave. When Shearman had not replied, Polglaze feared that the man might easily harm him or his sister, or possibly set fire to the ricks. He admitted that he ought to have fetched a policeman first, but hit him instead.

In summing up, the coroner said the jury had a choice of manslaughter, excusable homicide, justifiable homicide or wilful murder. They only retired for ten minutes before returning a verdict of wilful murder.

During his time in custody, he was examined on several occasions in October by the superintendent of the Cornwall County Lunatic Asylum. He said that in his view the prisoner was not of unsound mind, though he considered him to be of less than average ability.

The trial of Polglaze took place at Devon and Cornwall Assizes, Exeter, on 6 November, before Mr Baron Huddleston. Mr W. Molesworth St Aubyn and Mr J. Alderson Foote were counsel for the prosecution, while Mr Rockingham Gill appeared for the defence. Described by the *Western Morning News* as a well-built man, with a large greying beard, Polglaze appeared listless in court as he cast his eyes about. He gazed intently at the witnesses, especially his sister.

The medical officer at Bodmin Gaol, who had also examined Polglaze, considered him sane. His sister said that a nearby fire shortly before the incident had made him very nervous that something would happen to his hay. Charles Keast said he had always been a 'well-conducted', quiet, peaceable man, who regularly attended chapel and Sunday school. He did not 'mix up with no one', was 'a man to himself', and 'could not bear much to agitate him'. Constable Gill said that a man of excitable temperament seized with terror or frenzy had no control over his actions, but it would not amount to madness. In other words, he was sure Polglaze knew exactly what he was doing when he deliberately killed the man.

No witnesses were called for the defence, but it was urged that the prisoner was not guilty of the crime with which he stood charged.

In summing up for the prosecution, Mr St Aubyn asked how anybody could say that the prisoner was a man of unsound mind. Was it likely that, at the time he struck the blow, he did not know what the result would be? Speaking for himself, he would be very pleased if the jury could in all conscience say that the prisoner was out of his mind at the time. If they could not, Polglaze was surely guilty of cold-blooded murder.

For the defence, Mr Gill said that it was clear from the evidence that the prisoner had taken an axe, not for the purpose of revenge or for committing an unlawful act, but merely in self-defence. Even the policeman did not know who, or what, was under the hay. As soon as Polglaze saw the dark object concealed in the barn, he was overcome with a sense of fear. It was essential for his and for his sister's safety 'that this object should be removed'.

The judge pointed out that the prisoner had always admitted that he had caused the death of the deceased. The question for the jury was whether he was guilty of murder or manslaughter, and whether he was insane or not at the time. Following this, the judge then expanded on the law applicable to the case, and reviewed the evidence which had been given in court.

After retiring for three-quarters of an hour, the jury found him guilty, but strongly recommended mercy. In arrest of judgment, the prisoner said it was all through fright, and that he did not intend to hurt the deceased. The judge said he feared the prisoner, a man of a 'morose disposition', had cruelly and brutally beaten out the deceased's brains. He would take care that the recommendation of the jury should be forwarded to the proper quarter, but nevertheless passed sentence of death on the prisoner in the usual form.

In commenting on the verdict, the *Daily News* said that, 'To make Polglaze mount the gallows for this crime would only be to imitate his own unreasoning cruelty. He must be incurably stupid to be quite responsible for his act.'

However, Polglaze never mounted the gallows. On 11 November a notice of respite was received by Mr Stevens, the chief warder at Bodmin Gaol. The facts of the case suggested that he was probably no cold-blooded murderer; the findings of the authorities that he was 'not of average ability', coupled with the fact that he feared the trespasser was armed and could kill him, suggested a major element of self-defence. At the back of his mind must have been the thought that if he did not attack the trespasser, which could have been a person or wild creature, he or his sister might have been attacked instead – and fatally. Furthermore, he had admitted to the police that he had killed the man. Although he might have been sent to a lunatic asylum, or possibly discharged, the likelihood is that his sentence was commuted to imprisonment.

18

'DROWN
WILLIAM JOHN'

Newlyn, 1900

On the afternoon of 14 February 1900, seven-year-old William John Maddern – the son of Edwin Maddern, a fish hawker of Feradglan, near Newlyn – returned home from school as usual. He was looking forward to the evening as his school had organised a party for the children, complete with a bonfire. His twelve-year-old sister Fanny was going to come with him, and when they left the house together a little later he was quite excited.

Unhappily, it was the last treat he would ever have. When Fanny came back to the house that evening she was on her own. The next day William's dead body was found floating in the seaweed by fishermen in Newlyn Harbour. It was apparent that he had drowned at Gwavas Quay, and later that week the jury, at an inquest at Newlyn, concluded that his death was almost certainly a tragic accident.

At first, nobody outside the family had any reason to assume otherwise. Eight months later, however, everyone in the neighbourhood was horrified to learn that William John had apparently been murdered. In October, Fanny went to live with her aunt, Mrs Wallis, at St Paul Churchtown. Fanny told her that, on that fateful night, she had been told to push her little brother over the quay, and threatened with dire consequences if she failed to carry out the command.

Mrs Wallis reported this to the police, and on 18 October Fanny was formally arrested. Two days later she appeared before the Penzance magistrates at the town hall, charged with murdering young William John. The building was crowded as details of the most unpleasant episode gradually unfolded. George Bodilly, who had only been instructed that morning, acting for the prosecution, applied for a remand.

Fanny burst into tears and wept loudly as her father stood at her side, trying to comfort her. Inspector Sparks told how the little boy had returned from school, gone out with his sister but not come back with her that night. His body, badly bruised, especially around the face, was found in the seaweed at Newlyn next day by some fishermen who were getting ready to go out to sea.

Once she had calmed down, Fanny Maddern said that on the night of 14 February she had asked her brother to go home with her as it became dark, but he kicked out at her and insisted he wanted to go to the beach instead. Despite her entreaties that he should stay with her, he ran off, and she never saw him alive again. The coroner's jury at the initial inquest had believed that he drowned when he accidentally fell over the steep cliff near the pier, and returned a verdict to this effect.

At the end of the brief hearing, the magistrates granted a remand, and on 25 October Fanny's stepmother Mary was arrested and charged with incitement to murder the boy. Once again, the courtroom at Penzance town hall was crowded as Mrs Maddern, holding her eight-month-old baby, and Fanny both appeared before the magistrates a second time. In contrast to the previous occasion, Fanny was smiling – a weight had evidently been lifted off her young shoulders. She was the first to be charged, and Mr Bodilly told the court that he had laid the facts of the case before the Treasury. They had decided not to present any evidence on her behalf, and she was therefore to be discharged at once. Nevertheless, he warned that it was possible she might be brought before the Bench when the case against her stepmother 'was gone into in quite another capacity'.

Mr Boase said he had been instructed by the Children's Society to defend the child. In view of the course of events, it was only necessary for him to say that the society was still willing to do all they could for her safety.

Newlyn Harbour, 1950s. (Authors' collection)

Both the defending and prosecuting counsels agreed that the child's aunt would be the best person to take care of her. Fanny Maddern's discharge was received with loud applause, all those present undoubtedly relieved that the little girl could now put the last few traumatic months behind her.

Next it was the turn of Mary Maddern to come forward and be charged with having feloniously, and with malice aforethought, aided, abetted, counselled and procured her stepdaughter Fanny to murder William John. On behalf of the prosecution, Mr Bodilly said he had been instructed to ask for a remand until Saturday next, 3 November.

On behalf of Mary Maddern, Mr Thomas said that certain evidence had just been brought to his knowledge which, if correct, would be 'an absolute and complete answer to the charge'. However, it made necessary the most careful investigation, and he should himself have asked for a remand. The case was therefore adjourned until Saturday.

When proceedings were resumed at the same venue that day, Mary Maddern was charged with having abetted, counselled and procured Fanny Maddern to murder the boy. Public interest was mounting in the case, and again the building was packed with spectators. Charles Mathews appeared for the Treasury while Mr W.T. Lawrance was defending.

Now she had been discharged, Fanny Maddern was the main witness for the prosecution. To an astonished Bench, jury and crowd, she revealed that on Monday 12 February, her stepmother had ordered her, 'Drown William John'. Here she began to cast doubts on her credibility when she initially said that her sister Hilda and brother Luther were present at the time. When questioned further she changed her story a little, saying that nobody else was present, but she thought her brother and sister could hear what her stepmother had said. To this extraordinary family command she had made no reply.

Fanny claimed that two days later, after William John had returned from school and had tea, her stepmother had sent him straight to bed, even though he was going to the school party. Maybe she was punishing him for some naughtiness and intended to deny him the treat. However, she apparently changed her mind, as soon afterwards she told him he could go out after all, and ordered him to get up and dress. As Fanny and the others left the house, her stepmother again said, 'Mind you drown William John before you come home for the night. If you don't, you shall have nothing to eat.' Mary then gave the little boy some twine with a bent pin on the end, telling him to go to Gwavas Quay and catch some fish for her breakfast.

While they were out, Fanny continued, she found her brother on the quay, which had no rails. She came up behind him quickly, put her hand on his shoulder, and pushed him into the water. Although she did not hear any splash, she was confident that she had carried out the terrible deed as instructed, and went home immediately. When she arrived, she did not say anything to her stepmother, brother or sister. As William John failed to come indoors that night, her stepmother told all the children to search for him. Her sister Hilda, she said, had told the inquest in February that she had left her brother safe and sound at the playground; this was untrue, Mary Maddern had told her to make this false statement.

Mr Mathews pointed out that the deceased had been insured, and the Salvation Army had paid the family £5 on his death.

When called to the witness box, Hilda Maddern said that on the night of 13 February, she heard her stepmother say to Fanny, 'You must drown William John. I will give you a penny if you do it.' Then Fanny was told to go and see whether the tide was still in. She also heard Mary Maddern threaten to kill Fanny if she did not obey the order, at which Fanny said, 'All right,' and then went out. She came in again not long afterwards, telling her stepmother that the tide was not in far enough, and the sea was too shallow. Mrs Maddern remained obdurate.

'Unless you do it by Wednesday night,' she snapped, 'I will kill you.'

On the day of the tragedy, Hilda continued, she saw the prisoner go to a chest of drawers in the bedroom, take out some clean clothes for the boy, rouse him from his bed and get him dressed. Once more she repeated her instructions to Fanny, telling the girl that she was to push him over the quay, or she would kill her. The children then went out to see the bonfire, and after a while Fanny and her brother went away together. She saw Fanny get behind him and push him deliberately with both hands; on hearing a splash, she ran to the quay and saw the boy in the water. When she arrived home, her stepmother ordered her to search for her missing brother. She returned home alone and heard her stepmother ask Fanny if she had pushed her brother over; the answer was yes.

When her father returned later that night, Mary Maddern told him that William John was lost. He had gone to the playground to see the bonfire but never returned. Hilda was afraid to tell her father the truth, but after Fanny had been arrested and was in custody, she was so upset that she told her aunt, Mrs Carne, the whole story.

Several close neighbours of the Madderns were called. They said that they had heard Mrs Maddern say to Fanny, 'You drowned your little brother, didn't you? If you don't mind I will have you put away.' A policeman who had seen the boy after his body was recovered from the water described the clothes he was wearing, and said that they corresponded with the description given of his best clothes. He had had a bruise on his forehead and on the bridge of his nose. The prisoner denied that the boy was insured, but police evidence showed that he had been insured for £5 ten months before his death.

The magistrates retired to consider the evidence, and within half an hour returned to announce their intention of committing the prisoner for trial at Bodmin Assizes. In giving his consent, the chairman remarked that the case presented circumstances of difficulty which needed to be investigated by a jury.

On 9 November the case was heard before Mr Justice Ridley. He asked what evidence there was to corroborate the story, as no depositions had been taken by the coroner at the time. Not until people began to gossip several months after the sad event, he said, was there any suspicion that the boy's death might have been murder rather than an accident. There had been contradictory accounts of the same occurrence by Fanny and Hilda Maddern, throwing the greatest doubt possible on the truth of the allegation. It was a case of 'much suspicion', and he doubted whether they had reached the bottom of it. A further inquiry by the coroner might be ordered by the Attorney-General if he thought fit to do so, but if the Grand Jury took his (the judge's) view of the matter, they would think there was no case made out or deposition upon which the accused should be tried.

The Grand Jury accordingly passed a motion that in their opinion, 'the interests of justice demand a further inquiry in the coroner's court into the charge against Mary Maddern', and she was released.

As Mr Justice Ridley said, they had not reached 'the bottom of it', and they never did. It is hard to avoid the conclusion that little William John was murdered. Was Mary Maddern an evil stepmother, as portrayed by Fanny and Hilda, responsible for his death? Or did the sisters have a grudge against her, and conspire to sacrifice the unsuspecting boy in the hope that she might be convicted and removed from their lives forever by being sent to prison, or maybe even to the gallows? The Newlyn mystery was destined to remain a mystery.

19

'I SAW AN OLD MAN RUN AWAY FROM THE YARD'

Mount Hawke, 1901

At the turn of the century, infanticide, where the victim was over the age of one year, was often easier to prove than the murder of a newborn, as accidental death could generally be ruled out. Where the former was concerned, the mental state and general level of intelligence of the mother was often a crucial factor, especially if it reached court and a jury was called on to give judgment.

A prime example is the story of Ellen Phillips, a charwoman at Mount Hawke in 1901. An unmarried mother, she and her daughter Mary Elizabeth lived with her mother Elizabeth and sister. All three women took it in turns to look after the child while the other two went out to work.

Elizabeth Phillips had fallen on hard times. Her husband was a well-educated, successful businessman and mine owner who had died in unexplained circumstances some years earlier from a gunshot wound in Chile. It was rumoured that he might have taken his own life, but an air of mystery hung over the business, and nobody ever knew whether his death had been deliberate or accidental. Unfortunately for his family, he had left his considerable fortune in South America, and they never saw a penny of it.

Back in Cornwall, Elizabeth and her family had to adjust to circumstances as best they could. Their humdrum, but reasonably contented, life was shattered on 19 August 1901 when Elizabeth's granddaughter, two-year-old Mary, died. Owing to contradictory statements by Ellen Phillips herself, and the fact that not all of the witnesses could account for the exact time of events in their depositions to the court, precisely what occurred that day is still unclear.

According to Elizabeth Phillips, she and her other daughter (whose name never appeared in any subsequent report) went to work that morning, leaving Ellen and little Mary together at home, where they stayed until about midday. At about half past one Ellen met her mother 'in an excited state' as the latter was walking back from the vicarage, to tell her that little Mary Elizabeth had drowned. She then led her mother to Goosewartha, a deserted nearby farm. In the yard near a pump was a tub of water covered with a piece of sacking. Elizabeth removed this and found the dead, but still warm, body of her granddaughter. She immediately took the child out and attempted artificial respiration – but it was too late. When she asked Ellen, the latter said that she had missed the child, gone to look for it, and had seen a man running away. She had noticed the child's hat lying on the ground beside the tub, lifted up the cover, and on seeing the little body inside immediately went to look for her mother. Elizabeth doubtless wondered why her daughter had merely replaced the sacking, when surely her natural instinct would have been to remove the body from the water before doing anything else.

As they walked home, Ellen told her mother that she had not seen her daughter since ten o'clock. The Phillips family were well known in the Mount Hawke area and, despite her statement, several people had seen Ellen walking around outside with young Mary between midday and about one o'clock. About an hour later, Elizabeth and Ellen were back home with the body of the dead child. Several friends were also there, having presumably gathered partly out of curiosity and partly to commiserate.

Mount Hawke. (Authors' collection)

One woman, Dora Mary Brown, had known Mary ever since she was born. At the inquest at Truro two days later, she testified to having seen the child alone in Mount Hawke at about 12.45, walking in the direction of her home. She also reported that when they were at the house in the afternoon Elizabeth had said to her daughter reproachfully, 'Ellen, I hope you have not been in a temper.' 'Oh no,' was Ellen's answer. 'I saw an old man run away from the yard.' The implication was that a stranger had killed her little daughter, and then fled. Another friend, Amelia Ann Julyan, had asked, 'Why didn't you shriek to him?'

'I was crying so,' was Ellen's response, 'I couldn't make a sound.' When Amelia asked if she could give a description of the man, Ellen shook her head. 'I don't know whether he had a hard hat on or no, or whiskers or not; but he had cloth clothes on.' Amelia subsequently pointed out than there were bruises on the right side of the child's face, which prompted Elizabeth to ask Ellen if she had beaten the girl. The mother appeared horrified at the thought that anybody should believe her capable of ill-treatment. 'Oh! No, I never beat my child; I kissed it this morning. I took it to church last Sunday week morn, and it was so quiet and good there.'

An inquest was held on 21 August, attended by friends and neighbours ready to say they had noticed Ellen Phillips and her child together on the fatal morning, shortly before they saw the youngster's dead body. Also present as a witness was Constable Benney, the local policeman to whom the matter had been reported. He confirmed that Mary's body had been found drowned in the tub which contained about 9in of water, and that after making full enquiries he had arrested Ellen, cautioning her in the usual way. He said that she denied killing her child, and declared she had not seen Mary since ten o'clock that morning.

A verdict of wilful murder against Ellen Phillips, whose age was given as thirty-two, was returned, and she was brought before the county magistrates at Bodmin on 5 September 1901. Mr G. Appleby Jenkins, who prosecuted on behalf of the Treasury, said that she was 'identified closely with the death of her child', that she had the child in her possession shortly before its death, and that the medical evidence would prove that violence had produced its death. In short, she was responsible.

As with the inquest, several witnesses from Mount Hawke were in court for the occasion, and most of them said that they had seen the mother and her daughter together on the morning of 19 August. One of them, William Henry Harris, added that Ellen and Mary were proceeding along the road together at about one o'clock, and the mother 'was tearing as if in a hurry'. Another, Emily Ann Vincent, said she was at the back of her house when she heard a peculiar noise coming from the direction of Goosewartha Farm, although she did not mention at what time this occurred. She looked over the gate which led to her house and saw Ellen Phillips carrying a hat. When she called out to ask her what the matter was, she thought she understood Ellen to say rather incoherently that somebody had drowned. Ellen then walked briskly to the vicarage and Emily followed her, a short distance behind. By the time the latter arrived there, Ellen and her mother were coming out of the gate together. Aware that something serious must have happened, Emily asked what was going on.

In despair Mrs Phillips replied that she was unable to get any sense out of her daughter, apart from the fact that the child had been drowned at Mrs Richards's farm, Goosewartha. Ellen and her mother then went to the farm together, and Emily made her way there by a different route. When she arrived she saw Elizabeth Phillips with the child by the cattle-house door, 'rolling it and pulling something out of her little mouth – some yellow stuff.' Ellen was pulling the child's pinafore, and saying, 'Mary 'Lizabeth, speak, speak.' Emily asked where the child was drowned, and Mrs Phillips said, 'In that tub, my dear, with a bag over it; but it was killed before put in that tub.'

Ellen, she said, was adamant that she'd seen an old man running away when she first came to the farm, and thought he must have killed her child. Her mother asked how he was dressed, and Ellen Phillips claimed not to know. 'But how came you here to search for the child?' the mother had asked. 'I got on top the wood hedge and spied the hat outside the tub,' said the prisoner. Mrs Phillips looked to Ellen and said, ''Tis a funny old story you are telling me about this man; you will have to tell Mr Benney, the policeman, when he comes – what kind of clothes he had on, and all about him.' Ellen replied helplessly that she could not, 'I don't know what kind of clothes he had, nor hat, nor whiskers.'

Constable Benney repeated the evidence he had given at the inquest, while Superintendent Bassett said that Ellen had reported the child missing at midday on 19 August. (This was despite William Harris's statement that he had seen mother and child an hour later.) When she went to look for Mary, she saw her hat beside a tub, covered with a bag, at Goosewartha Farm. She was sure her child was in the tub, and immediately ran to look for her mother.

After similar evidence was produced by other witnesses, the chairman committed her for trial at the next Bodmin Assizes, where she appeared on 16 November before Mr Justice Gainsford-Bruce. Mr F. Bodilly and Mr J.A. Simon prosecuted, and Mr J. Fraser Macleod appeared for the defence. Through her tears the prisoner pleaded 'Not Guilty' to murder.

For the prosecution, Mr Bodilly said that although the evidence against her was purely circumstantial, it all pointed 'irresistibly' to Ellen Phillips having killed her child. At eight o'clock on the morning of the child's death, the prisoner's mother and sister went out to work, while she remained alone with her until about midday. The mother, who was working at the vicarage, near her house, saw nothing more of Ellen until about half-past one when she arrived in an excited state, telling her that Mary Elizabeth had drowned. They went to Goosewartha where they found the tub of water covered with sacking in the yard. Elizabeth Phillips found the dead body of the child in the water, and tried in vain to resuscitate her. When asked about it, Ellen told her mother she was looking for her missing child, and had seen a man run away. She also said she saw the child's hat by the tub, concluded that the child was dead, lifted up the cover, saw the child inside, replaced the sacking, then went to her mother.

Despite the evidence of witnesses, Ellen still told her mother she had not seen Mary since ten o'clock in the morning, and repeated this to Charles Harris and Constable Benney. The next day, in conversation with the police sergeant, she changed her story,

Assize court in Bodmin, 1950s.
(Authors' collection)

saying she did not see the child after midday. If she had not seen her child after that hour, the evidence might not have been strong enough to justify the jury in finding the prisoner guilty. But between 12.45 and 12.50, Mrs Annie Rogers saw Ellen Phillips at the end of the road in the village with the child, and at one o'clock Ellen was seen with the child by Mrs Boyle as the latter returned from Gover Farm. Later she was seen again with the child by William Henry Harris and Eliza Jane Harris. All of these witnesses testified to having seen the accused woman walking in the direction of Goosewartha.

Medical evidence would prove that the child was not drowned. She had been suffocated and then immersed in the water, as the lungs were not filled with water and the bruises around the lower part of the face and neck suggested that pressure had been applied while she was still alive. It was significant that, when arrested, Ellen gave a different version of events to the police constable to what she had told her mother. To him she made no mention of another man, nor did she indicate that she had looked in the tub, but told him that when she found the child was missing, she went to look for her, and while she was searching in a field she saw the child's hat lying near the tub.

If this was correct, asked Mr Bodilly, what would make the prisoner think the child was drowned? The body would have probably been in the tub, but might have still been alive, so what prevented her from going there to see if she was able to save it? He submitted that the child must have died at the hands of the prisoner, and no other person was involved. While the prisoner said she saw a man running away, she had given no explanation, or tried to give any description of him. As to what became of him, or what happened in the few minutes the murder took place, she could suggest nothing, nor why the child should be murdered by a stranger at a moment's notice. There was no sign of outrage on the child, which was untouched except for suffocation marks, nor was there any evidence from others of a strange person having been seen in the neighbourhood at the time.

After James Henderson, a surveyor from Truro, had produced a map of the locality, a deeply affected Elizabeth Phillips gave her evidence. She said that when she left home that morning the child was in bed asleep, and her daughter was in charge. The next time she saw the latter, about 1.30, she was in tears, weeping for her little child who had just drowned. When Mrs Phillips asked how it could have happened, her daughter said she did not know. Mrs Phillips immediately dropped her work and tried to comfort her daughter, who was beginning to ramble, and talking so incoherently that it was almost impossible to understand her. At this stage the tub and sacking were produced in court, and the witness added that when she and Ellen were on their way to the farmyard, the latter said she had been searching for the child more than two hours.

Elizabeth Phillips then went to the tub, lifted up the sacking, and found it full of clear water. Mary's body was floating on the top and she took it out, asking the prisoner how it had happened. 'I don't know,' was the answer. 'When I got on the hedge I saw an old man pass the yard ... I expect that old man must have injured my child.' After failing to revive the child, Elizabeth took the body home and sent for a policeman.

Under cross-examination, she said there could be no fonder mother than her daughter, and they were all happy and comfortable at home. Ellen Phillips helped in trying to revive the child and begged Mary to speak to them. Mrs Phillips admitted that when her daughter was young she was not very bright, and not that strong intellectually now; she was nearly thirteen before she could speak and she had been very poorly educated. The prisoner's sister Mary was also very weak-minded. Since the mysterious death of her husband in South America, Ellen had been the mainstay of her house, and used to take her to church and chapel. She knew the difference between right and wrong, and had always been a very good daughter.

When she was questioned further by Mr Bodilly as to whether her daughter was weak-minded, she said, 'I don't think she could go through the world like some. She was very quiet, and fit to be trusted alone in looking after the house.'

Other witnesses then gave a similar version of events, among them various neighbours, as well as Constable Benney, Superintendent Bassett, Frederick Carlyon, the Truro physician who had helped carry out the post-mortem, and fellow surgeons William Whitworth and Bartholomew Derry. The latter, a medical officer at the prison, had had the prisoner under his care since her committal on 29 August; he had seen her twice every weekday and once on Sunday, invariably found her conversation rational, and considered her a woman of 'ordinary intelligence'. He noticed no signs of excitement or depression in her, apart from crying once or twice after seeing the chaplain, and did not think there was any suggestion of insanity.

For the prosecution, Mr Bodilly asked the jury to discount all medical evidence suggesting the prisoner suffered from an attack of homicidal mania when the offence was committed, as it was improbable that she could have had such an attack and be perfectly rational again in half an hour. For the defence, Mr Macleod told the jury that if they had any reasonable doubt as to whether the prisoner committed the murder, or whether, if she did it, she was not at the time responsible for her actions, to give her the benefit of the doubt. The prosecution had proved too much; there must be some mistake or fallacy with regard to the time, as no woman could have dragged a child three-quarters of a mile, killed it and then gone to the vicarage in half an hour. As the child was beloved by all the family, there was no obvious motive. Maybe the prisoner did not kill the child or, if she did, her mind was unhinged. If the jury considered she had killed her child while 'under the influence of an irresistible and uncontrollable impulse', and therefore did not know the difference between right and wrong, that would mean a verdict in her favour.

Summing up the case, the judge said the question of the jury was whether there was enough evidence to justify their belief that the child could only have met her death at the hands of the prisoner. If there was any truth in her story about a man running away, why did she not speak to him, or raise an alarm, or at least attempt to rescue the child? Should the jury be satisfied that the prisoner was last seen with the child before the body was found, and that her story was untrue, they must conclude that she put Mary in the tub herself. If they were satisfied that she caused the child's death, they would find her guilty, and if so, the question was whether she was responsible for her actions. If there was any mental delusion in this case, it did not manifest itself either before or after the crime, and it was for the jury to say whether she was responsible at the time for the act.

There were three possible verdicts. They might find the prisoner not guilty of committing the offence; they might say she did commit it, and was guilty of murder; or they might find that when she committed the act, she was so mentally deranged that she did not know the difference between right and wrong.

After retiring for twenty minutes, the jury returned with a verdict of 'Guilty'. The Clerk of Assize asked the prisoner whether she wished to say anything. 'I ain't guilty, sir,' she answered so softly that he had to ask her to repeat it.

After pausing, he donned the black cap, and was about to pass sentence of death when the foreman rose to ask, 'Did we not understand from your lordship that there was another verdict we could bring in?' Asked by the judge to continue, he went on, 'We consider that the prisoner was not of sufficiently sound mind as to know what she was doing when she committed the crime, and that she was not strong enough in her mind to resist the temptation and the impulse at the time.' In reply to a further question from the judge, he said they believed she did not know right from wrong. After the Clerk of the Assize confirmed that it was the verdict of them all, the judge sentenced her to be kept in Bodmin Gaol at His Majesty's pleasure. She was removed from court, and the judge told the jury that she would ultimately be taken to a lunatic asylum, where she could be properly treated.

20

'HOWEVER DID I COME TO DO IT?'

Penzance, 1901

Justinian Carter married Elizabeth Mary Harvey in January 1901 and on 13 October of that year she gave birth to the couple's first child. Since their marriage, Justinian and Mary, as she was usually known, had lived in St Michael's Street, Penzance with her mother and fourteen-year-old brother, Thomas. However, the birth of his baby daughter prompted Justinian to look for a home of his own and, when a cottage became vacant just a few doors away from his mother-in-law's house, he decided to take it.

Mary's father worked as a miner in South Africa and her mother, Elizabeth, was of a rather nervous disposition. She suffered from agoraphobia, hated going outside and also had bouts of chronic depression, insomnia and loss of appetite. She had come to rely heavily on her daughter and, on one occasion before Mary's marriage, had even insisted that Mary return home from a live-in job as an apprentice dressmaker because she so hated living alone. Elizabeth enjoyed having her daughter and son-in-law around the house and doted on her new granddaughter, but she did appreciate the young couple's need for a home of their own and gave them her blessing. 'Everyone is best in their own house,' she told Justinian on hearing of his intention to move. However, her apparent cheerfulness belied a terrible anxiety and Elizabeth stopped eating and sleeping, inwardly dreading the day when Mary would leave her. As the move approached, Elizabeth seemed to panic and begged Justinian to reconsider his decision. Although he had always got on well with his mother-in-law and there had been no quarrel between them, Justinian was understandably keen to have a place that he and his family could truly call home. He pointed out to Elizabeth that his new house was only a couple of doors away from hers and she would always be a welcome visitor.

The morning of 31 October started exactly the same way as every other morning in the house on St Michael's Street. Elizabeth was up early and made breakfast for Justinian, who left the house at just before nine o'clock to go to his job as a linotype operator. Thomas got ready for school and Elizabeth took a cup of tea and some toast up to Mary, who was still in bed. She asked her daughter if the baby had slept well, to which Mary replied that her daughter had been quite restless and had woken her several times during the night. Elizabeth offered to hold the baby, and sat in the bedroom for a few minutes with her granddaughter on her lap while Mary ate her breakfast.

Meanwhile, Thomas was dawdling in the kitchen and Elizabeth began to worry that he would be late for school. She shouted downstairs to ask if he had eaten his breakfast and, when Thomas answered 'No', Elizabeth told Mary that she would have to go down and sort him out, leaving the bedroom with the baby in a blanket in her arms.

When Elizabeth arrived in the kitchen, she asked Thomas to light the fire in the front room. As Thomas walked past his niece, he affectionately tickled the baby and Elizabeth beamed at him, asking 'Isn't she looking handsome?' Thomas agreed that she was and went to light the fire. When he returned to the kitchen, his mother said conversationally, 'I have killed the child.'

For a moment, Thomas could scarcely believe his own ears but then he saw his niece lying on the kitchen table, her throat cut from ear to ear and the tablecloth stained bright red with her blood. Thomas let out a horrified scream and Mary called worriedly from upstairs, asking what the matter was. 'Mary, I've killed your baby,' Elizabeth calmly shouted up to her.

Mary flew downstairs in her nightdress and snatched the baby from the kitchen table, running back upstairs to her bedroom in a state of hysterics, with Elizabeth and Thomas close behind her.

Elizabeth seemed dazed and confused, 'Whatever did I do it for?' she asked repeatedly. 'What have I done?'

Mary asked Thomas to fetch her father-in-law, Justinian Carter senior.

'How can I tell him mother's killed the baby?' asked Thomas, to which Mary told him just to say that the baby was dead.

Thomas ran out of the house, leaving Elizabeth and Mary alone in the bedroom together. 'What will they do to me?' Elizabeth fretted, constantly wringing her hands and pacing around the room. Somehow, Mary managed to talk calmly to her mother until Justinian Carter senior arrived with his wife, Faith, his son, and surgeons Dr Branwell and Dr Bennett. The two doctors quickly established that they could do nothing to help the baby, whose head had been almost severed from her body with a bread knife. As Mr and Mrs Carter senior tried to comfort their grief-stricken son and daughter-in-law, the doctors turned their attention to Elizabeth Harvey, who still seemed completely bewildered by what had happened.

In answer to their questions, she told the doctors that she had felt unwell for some time and that she had a 'heavy gloom' upon her. She professed she was unable to sleep properly, saying that she felt restless and couldn't settle to anything. She repeatedly asked, 'However did I come to do it?' telling the doctors that she had not known what she was doing at the time.

The police were called and Superintendent Nicholas took fifty-two-year-old Elizabeth Harvey into custody, 'I hope and trust they will not hang me,' she told Nicholas, continuing to insist, 'I don't know what made me do it.'

Elizabeth was brought before magistrates charged with the wilful murder of her granddaughter, who, at just eighteen days old, had not yet even been given a name. She was remanded in custody on the understanding that she would be examined by a doctor to determine her mental state. On the same day, an inquest into the baby's death was opened by coroner Mr G.L. Bodilly.

Justinian Carter and Thomas Harvey told the inquest that, on the morning of the murder, Elizabeth's behaviour had seemed completely normal. However, they related that she was very upset about the fact that Mary and Justinian were moving out. Dr Charles Branwell stated that, after examining the baby on the morning of the murder, he and Dr Bennett had spoken at length to Elizabeth Harvey. Although she was relatively calm and able to speak rationally, Branwell said that he had formed the impression that the thought of separation from her daughter had been preying heavily on her mind and, at what the doctor called 'this critical time of her life', this anxiety could have induced a spontaneous fit of homicidal mania. Since Mary Carter was too ill to attend the proceedings, the coroner adjourned the inquest for two weeks after hearing from Dr Branwell, in the hope that Mary would have sufficiently recovered by then to testify.

Penzance. (Authors' collection)

Mary was indeed able to appear at the resumed inquest and, having related the events of the morning of 31 October, she too stated that her mother had seemed particularly despondent when she and Justinian announced their intention of setting up home with the baby. Questioned further about her mother's mental state by Mr J. Vivian Thomas, the solicitor who was attending the inquest on behalf of Elizabeth Harvey, Mary admitted that her mother had a long history of depression and insomnia and often became excessively anxious about the smallest of things. Mary recalled that when she was a very small child, Elizabeth had once tried to put her in the oven and, as a result, she had spent some time living with her grandparents.

Justinian's mother, Faith Carter, told the inquest that Mrs Harvey was normally a very pleasant woman but was occasionally somewhat strange in her ways. Elizabeth had told her that she suffered greatly with headaches and sometimes she just had to go outside and let it rain on her head to ease the pain. Mrs Carter confirmed that Elizabeth had been distraught at the idea of Mary moving out of her home and had told her, 'I don't believe I can live without Mary.'

Everyone agreed that Elizabeth had a good relationship with her daughter and son-in-law and was an especially doting grandmother to the baby she had so nearly decapitated.

Having heard all the witnesses, the inquest jury retired for a few minutes before returning with a verdict of wilful murder against Elizabeth Harvey. However, foreman Mr P. Chirgwin was keen to ensure that the coroner was aware of the jury's unanimous belief that she had committed the murder during a temporary attack of insanity. Mr Bodilly told them that it was not within the remit of the inquest to determine Mrs Harvey's mental state at the time of the murder but nevertheless he promised that he would add such a rider to their verdict. Bodilly then committed Elizabeth Harvey for trial at the next Assizes.

Her trial opened at Bodmin before Mr Justice Channell in November 1901, with Mr McKellar and Mr Fraser MacLeod prosecuting and Mr Frank Bodilly acting as defence counsel. McKellar opened the proceedings by describing the events of the morning of 31 October leading up to what he called 'this horrible and barbarous murder'. Saying that the defendant had seemed particularly fond of her first grandchild, McKellar admitted that the main issue to concern the jury would be the condition of Mrs Harvey's mind at the time of the offence.

Mary and Justinian Carter, Thomas Harvey, Justinian Carter senior and his wife, Faith, all gave exactly the same testimony as they had given at the inquest. They were followed into the witness box by Drs Branwell and Bennett, who spoke of being summoned to St Michael's Street in the wake of the baby's murder. Both doctors had formed the opinion that Elizabeth Harvey had not known what she was doing at the time, as had Superintendent Nicholas, who had been promoted to Chief Constable by the time of the trial.

The defence called Dr J.H. Tonkin, a Camborne doctor who had treated Elizabeth Harvey before her move to Penzance a year or so before the tragedy. Tonkin told

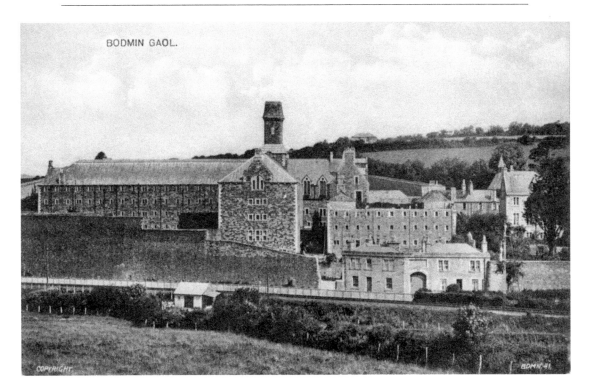

BODMIN GAOL.

Bodmin Gaol. (Authors' collection)

the court that Elizabeth suffered from a history of depression, insomnia and melancholia. Tonkin was followed into the witness box by Dr Bartholomew Derry, the medical officer for Bodmin Gaol, where Elizabeth had been confined since the murder.

Dr Derry told the court that Elizabeth had never been able to offer any explanation as to why she had killed her beloved granddaughter. She insisted that when she left the bedroom and took the baby downstairs, she had no intention of harming her, but said that as soon as she saw the bread knife, something told her that she had to use it to kill the baby. Based on his observations of Elizabeth during her incarceration, and judging by what he had heard from Drs Bennett, Branwell and Tonkin, Dr Derry was prepared to state that Elizabeth Harvey was insane at the time of the murder.

Thus the jury's verdict was perhaps a foregone conclusion – they found Elizabeth Harvey 'guilty' of the wilful murder of her granddaughter but determined that, in the eyes of the law, she was insane at the time and therefore not responsible for her actions. Mr Justice Channell ordered her to be confined in Bodmin Gaol during His Majesty's pleasure.

Note: In contemporary accounts of the case, the surgeon who attended on the morning of the murder is referred to as both Dr Bennett and Dr Bennetts.

21

'LISTEN ... HE'S MURDERING THE CHILDREN'

Saltash, 1901

Mrs Bertha Palmer nudged her husband Charles awake in the early hours of the morning of 21 August 1901. 'Listen,' she urged him, 'he's murdering the children.'

Charles Palmer heard what sounded suspiciously like gunshots coming from the home of Henry Thomas Mortimer, their neighbour in Home Park Road, Saltash. Resignedly, he started to get up to investigate the noises but Mrs Palmer pulled him back.

'Don't go,' she begged, telling her husband that it was too dangerous and she was afraid to be left alone. Palmer gradually calmed his wife down. He reminded Bertha that their neighbour had recently made some fireworks and was most probably just discharging them. He had spoken to Mortimer only that day and their neighbour had seemed perfectly normal, telling Palmer that he was moving away to live in Southampton the following month. Palmer reassured his wife that there was no reason to suspect that Mortimer's children were in any danger – their father had been happily playing with them just hours earlier. Having succeeded in convincing themselves that Mortimer was only letting off fireworks, the Palmers managed to go back to sleep.

Unusually, when the Palmers woke up the next morning, there were no signs of life from the house next door, which was occupied by Mortimer, his wife Georgina, and their four young children. As the day wore on, the house remained suspiciously quiet and, as night fell and no lights appeared in the windows, the Palmers became sufficiently concerned to contact the police.

When the police officer who arrived was unable to rouse anybody within the house, he procured a ladder, which he placed up against a first-floor balcony. On entering the premises, he was met by a horrific sight.

In the front bedroom, Georgina Mortimer, aged about thirty-three, lay dead on the bed, half of her face obliterated by a shotgun blast. On either side of the bed was a cot containing the bodies of three-year-old Kennedy and five-year-old Madge. Each of the children had been shot in the head. Henry Mortimer lay on the floor at the foot of the bed, a double-barrelled shotgun still resting between his legs. The muzzle pointed towards what remained of his head, which had been shot almost completely from his body, leaving only his chin intact. In the back bedroom, nine-year-old Eric was found kneeling close to the door, his arm thrown over a chair, while his younger brother, Alan, aged seven, was spreadeagled on the floor. Like their younger siblings, both boys had been shot in the head.

Above: *Saltash, 1909. (Authors' collection)*

Left: *Home Park Road, Saltash. (© Kim Van der Kiste)*

An inquest was opened into the deaths at the Railway Hotel, Saltash, by coroner Mr A.C.L. Glubb. Having heard evidence from Charles Palmer and Dr Meadow, who had attended the scene and subsequently performed post-mortem examinations on the six deceased, Glubb adjourned the proceedings. He was in receipt of a telegram from Rundle and Jackson, a firm of solicitors from Devonport, who had acted for Mortimer for several years. Partner Mr J.S.B. Jackson believed that he was in possession of several facts pertinent to the investigation and, when the inquest reopened the next day, it was with Jackson as the main witness.

Jackson told the inquest that Henry Thomas Mortimer was originally from Watford in Hertfordshire but had been banished to Saltash by his family, since he was something of an embarrassment to them, due to what was referred to as '… an inability to control his loose morals'. A keen sportsman and an active member of the local rifle club, Mortimer was a man of private means and Jackson was confident that his financial situation at the time of his death was healthy. However, Georgina Mortimer was, in fact, Georgina Luscombe. Although she and Henry had lived together as man and wife for many years and produced four children together, they were not legally married. Jackson believed that this was because Mortimer was already married to another woman and that his first wife was still alive, although her present whereabouts were unknown.

An intelligent man, Mortimer was thought of as an eccentric who held rather radical views on most subjects including religion, politics and society in general. He was described as 'outside in all his views' and his religious beliefs were such that he did not entertain the idea of heaven – or any afterlife.

Mortimer was a man of great contrasts. Although he was a sober man, he was said to have an 'uncertain temper'. He was devoted to his 'wife' and children but, at the same time, he seemed totally incapable of sexual fidelity and apparently had several affairs. In April, a woman named Hodge had served him with an affiliation summons, alleging that he was the father of her illegitimate child and seeking maintenance. Jackson had settled this claim on his client's behalf and told the inquest that he had also settled a previous similar claim. There was also a suggestion that Mortimer had been sexually involved with a female servant in his household.

The inquest jury's verdict was a foregone conclusion and they quickly determined that Charles Henry Mortimer had murdered his common-law wife and four children and then committed *felo de se* (an archaic term, literally meaning 'felon of himself', historically used to denote suicides). What was less clear was his motive for doing so and whether or not he had been sane at the time of the shootings.

The coroner advanced several theories. Mortimer was 'a bad man', who inwardly felt undeserving of what everyone described as '… such nice little children'. In shooting each of his family members in the head, Mortimer had apparently tried to make their deaths as quick and humane as possible. Was Mortimer afraid that his children might inherit his own evil tendencies? Were the killings altruistic, or even profoundly compassionate, in that Mortimer had come to believe that his family would be better off dead than living with him as their husband and father? With no firm beliefs or faith, Mortimer's actions would not have been tempered by any religious considerations.

Undoubtedly a clever man, with a sound intellect, Mortimer was also a man with a highly emotional temperament. Had something unusual happened in the house prior to the murders, which had so affected Mortimer's emotions that they had overridden his intellect and rendered him incapable of controlling them?

The coroner described Mortimer as a gentleman, stating that he had none of the tendencies of 'truculence and barbarity' that the nature of his acts might suggest. Whatever else he was, he was not a ferocious man and the shootings had not been carried out with ferocious intent. Yet everyone who had spoken to him prior to the brutal slaying of his entire family believed him to be entirely sane and, as far as anyone was aware, he had no personal or familial history of insanity or mental illness.

Dr Meadow could only say that he believed the shootings to be the result of an insane impulse. The fact that the shootings occurred at around 3.15 a.m. and that Mortimer alone had been fully dressed, while the rest of his family had been in their night attire, suggested that he had probably sat alone in the house for several hours after everyone else had retired for the night, brooding and thinking about his actions.

The funerals of the Mortimer family were held at St Stephens by Saltash on the day after the inquest. Georgina Luscombe was conveyed to her final resting place in a glass hearse, along with two small coffins, each of which contained the bodies of two of her children. After a simple ceremony, conducted by the vicar of Saltash, Revd A. Preedy, the three coffins were lowered into a shared grave.

The large but silent crowd who had attended the funeral lingered by the graveside after the service had ended and the vicar had left and, an hour later, the body of Henry Thomas Mortimer arrived at the churchyard and was placed in the same grave. This time there was no ceremony or religious service and no wreaths of flowers adorned the plain wooden coffin. As they had been united in life, the Mortimer family were forever united in death.

St Stephens by Saltash. (© Kim Van der Kiste)

In the minds of everyone connected to the case, important questions remained unanswered. Why should Henry Thomas Mortimer find it necessary to shoot the partner and children he apparently idolised before taking his own life? What could have happened to change him in a matter of hours from a loving father, happily playing with his children, to someone who would calmly and deliberately obliterate himself and his entire family with six shots from a shotgun? Yet the question that haunted many people was whether or not there had been any warning signs – could the tragedy have been predicted and so prevented?

Note: There is some confusion about the name of the Mortimers' youngest child. Some contemporary sources give the boy's name as either Hags or Hago K. Mortimer. The 'K' apparently stands for Kennedy, the name by which he was known in the family, and the child's correct first name appears to have been Hugo.

22

'REST, DEAR MAID, WHERE KIND FRIENDS HAVE LAID THEE'

Castle an Dinas, 1904

Castle an Dinas near St Columb is an ancient fort, perched high on the top of a hill and, on a clear day, the views from the summit are spectacular, attracting visitors all year round to gaze across the countryside as far as the Bristol and English Channels. Thus, when two brothers named Tabb spotted a young man and woman cycling along the main road towards the fort on Saturday, 11 June 1904, they took no particular notice. They watched the couple park their cycles in a gateway and head off on foot towards the summit of the hill, laughing and chatting as they went. However, at eleven o'clock the next morning, their bicycles were still in the gateway and obviously hadn't been moved since the previous evening.

Mr Tabb and his brother moved both cycles to a safer place before setting off to see if they could find any trace of the young couple who had been riding them. They climbed the hill until they came to the three circular entrenchments at its peak. Just inside the outermost circle, they were shocked to find the body of the young lady they had seen behaving in such a happy and carefree manner only the evening before. She lay on her back on the grass, drenched in blood, her arms crossed over her chest and her face terribly disfigured by bullet wounds.

The Tabb brothers sent a message to the police station at St Columb and, before long Inspector Nicholls and PC Collett arrived at the scene. Examining the body, they noticed that the girl's skin and parts of her hair were singed, from which they concluded that the gunshots that killed her had been fired at close range.

Left: *Castle an Dinas.*
(Authors' collection)

Below: *St Mawgan.*
(Authors' collection)

Nicholls arranged for the body to be taken to the police station at St Columb, where it was found that the young girl had been shot six times, once in her left arm, once in her left cheek, twice near to her left eye, once in her neck and once behind her left ear. She was examined by Dr Mackey, who was quite sure that she would have died instantly as a result of her injuries.

Meanwhile, Mr Pascoe Rickard of St Columb Major was desperately searching for his seventeen-year-old daughter, Jessie. On the previous evening, Jessie had left home to cycle to St Mawgan, where she intended to visit a friend, Miss Berryman, from whom she was receiving music lessons. She had promised to meet her father at St Columb at ten o'clock in the evening and, although he was at their appointed meeting place in good time and waited almost an hour for his daughter, she never arrived.

Thinking that Jessie had decided to stay overnight with her friend, Mr Rickard eventually went home. The next morning, when there was still no sign of Jessie, he went to St Mawgan to see what had become of her and was horrified to learn that she wasn't there. More worrying still was the fact that Miss Berryman's brother, Charles, had also been out all night.

By then, the police had retrieved the two bicycles and, on searching the basket of the woman's bicycle, found a wallet containing a photograph of Jessie Rickard. Since the badly disfigured corpse at the police station bore no resemblance to the pretty, smiling girl in the photograph, the officers wrongly assumed that the dead girl must have been a friend of Jessie's and called in her half-brother, Everett Rickard, to see if he could name her. Everett was appalled to find that the body was that of his own half-sister and he then had the unenviable task of breaking the dreadful news of Jessie's murder to her father.

With the dead girl's name now known, the police began a search for her missing companion, Charles Berryman.

A description was circulated to all the local newspapers:

Wanted, for the wilful murder of Miss Jessie Rickard at Castle an Dinas, St Columb on the 11th inst. Charles Berryman of St Mawgan, carpenter, aged twenty years. Height 5ft 3-4in, medium build, light brown hair, full face, fair complexion, blue eyes, dressed in dark cloth suit with small white stripe running through, grey skull cap, white linen collar turned down all round, necktie tied in a sailor's knot, brown boots. He has a brother residing at 23 Bellevue Crescent, Cockington, Torquay and another at 51 Melrose Road, Eston, Norwich. Berryman will most likely try to leave the country.

As soon as people heard that Berryman was missing, they flocked to Castle an Dinas in droves to assist in the hunt for him, which was being directed by Superintendent Bassett from Truro. The entire area was searched with some difficulty since it was wild, rough scrub land and there were numerous places where a man might hide if he wanted to avoid discovery. The searchers probed bogs, hacked through gorse bushes and bracken, peered into farm buildings and abandoned mines and waded through ditches and streams, all the while hampered by torrential rain. On Monday afternoon, dynamite was deployed in several ponds and flooded mineshafts to encourage the corpse to float to the surface if Berryman had drowned himself.

Berryman had often talked about going to America and the police were consequently afraid that he might flee the country. On Monday afternoon, a rumour spread like wildfire that his body had been found in a pond on Goss Moor. The police were quick to deny this and also a second rumour that a young man had been found shot dead near Liskeard. Several people came forward purporting to have seen Berryman in the vicinity, including a group of workmen who approached a man near St Columb on Monday morning. It was suggested that he might have caught a train to Plymouth, or that he might have fled to the homes of one of his two brothers in Cockington or Norwich. Berryman had served his apprenticeship as a carpenter in Torquay and was thus very familiar with the region, although given the publicity surrounding his disappearance, the police believed that he would probably avoid going to an area where he would be instantly recognised.

When the police interviewed Berryman's family they discovered that, when he left the house, he only had seven pence in his pocket, although he had around £5 in his bedroom. His sister had actually asked him before he set out if he needed money and Charles had checked his trouser pocket, saying, 'I have left mine upstairs. But I find I have seven pence and I shall not want anything.' Thus, assuming that he did not have the financial means to travel far, the police continued to focus their search for Berryman around Castle an Dinas.

The Red Lion, St Columb. (© N. Sly)

An inquest into the death of Jessie Rickard was opened at the Red Lion Hotel in St Columb, on the Monday after the discovery of her body. Coroner Mr R.F. Edyvean stated that he wished to spare Mr Rickard as much pain as possible and therefore proposed to hear only evidence of identity and the medical evidence before adjourning the inquest to await further developments, which would at least allow Rickard to hold a funeral for his daughter.

It was the duty of the coroner's jury to inspect the body and, being local men, most of them had known Jessie. Her features almost destroyed by bullets, many of the jurors found it difficult to believe that this was all that was left of the happy, vivacious young girl who they had always known as '... such a bright little thing', and several remarked upon the expression of pain and terror etched on what was left of her once beautiful face. Yet, however horrific Jessie's death had been, the coroner was able to give her grieving father one small crumb of comfort – surgeon Dr Mackey had been able to confirm that, although Jessie's clothing had been disturbed, she had not been raped and had died a virgin.

'Thank God! Thank God!' sobbed the distraught Mr Rickard on hearing the news.

Jessie's funeral was held two days later, her white coffin carried to her grave by members of the St Columb String Band. Hundreds of mourners lined her route to the cemetery, braving the pouring rain to accompany her to her final resting place. The local newspapers printed a particularly apt memorial notice: 'In Memoriam (Jessie): Rest, dear maid, where kind friends have laid thee, May God forgive him who betrayed thee – to an awful tragic doom, mid thy young life's early bloom. (W. Street)'

On the following day, Berryman's body was finally found in a pool on the north side of the hill at Castle an Dinas. There was a single bullet wound in his forehead and, when the police dragged the pool, they recovered a revolver.

In his pocket was a photograph of Jessie, along with a letter addressed to his mother dated 12 June and headed 'St Columb'. The letter, which gave instructions for the disposal of Berryman's possessions, was signed 'I remain your affectionate son, Charley'. At Berryman's inquest on 17 June, Mr Edyvean informed the jury that, although the letter was dated 12 June, it appeared to have been written by somebody who was quite calm and collected and it did not seem to have been written outside. He questioned whether the letter had been written on or before Saturday, pointing out that, if that was the case then the only conclusion that could be drawn was that Miss Rickard's murder was premeditated.

Nobody had been aware that Charles Berryman owned a revolver and it emerged at the inquest that he had purchased the gun and fifty bullets from a shop in Truro the day before the murder. The wounds inflicted on Jessie Rickard and Charles Berryman had been caused by a very small gun, which was described as 'little more than a toy'. It was only the fact that the gun had been fired at such close range that had made it a lethal weapon and, according to the coroner, this suggested a very determined assailant.

There had been 'an amorous attachment' between Charles Berryman and Jessie Rickard, although it had obviously been more serious for Charles than for Jessie,

Charles Berryman and Jessie Rickard. (© N. Sly)

since she was seen on the Wednesday prior to her death on the beach at St Mawgan in the company of a young man from St Columb. Although nobody could ever be certain of the reasons behind Charles Berryman's actions on 11 June, it was theorised that they had been precipitated by jealousy.

The inquests into the deaths of Jessie Rickard and Charles Berryman were finally brought to a conclusion on 20 June 1904. The coroner's jury first returned a verdict of 'wilful murder by Charles Berryman' on the death of Jessie Rickard, followed by a verdict of *felo de se* on her killer, to which the jury added a rider stating that they could find no evidence of insanity.

23

'TELL THEM THAT I DID IT'

Tregothnan, 1904

Over the years, many a man has been killed while out hunting or shooting for sport. More often than not the death was accidental, although sometimes there were grave doubts as to whether or not the killing was premeditated. There can be few better ways for the determined to commit 'the perfect murder' than by taking aim at their intended victim in such circumstances, the most famous instance in England being the death (or possible assassination) of King William II in the New Forest in August 1100. A lesser-known, more recent example occurred in Cornwall some 800 years later.

Henry Osmond, who lived at Merther, was an under-gamekeeper who had been employed since the early summer of 1903 by Viscount Falmouth on his Tregothnan estate, his main duty being to watch the estate and warn off any poachers. At about 2 p.m. on the afternoon of 25 January he said goodbye to his wife Maria and left the house, accompanied by his dog and taking a gun. A few hours later he was seen, near Nancemabyn Wood, by two separate people who passed him as he was on his way home.

They were the last people to set eyes on him while he was still alive. As he failed to return home that night, a search party led by Constable Baker went out the next day to look for him. At about 2.30 p.m. one of the men saw and recognised the under-gamekeeper's dog by an oak tree, and called out to the others. On the west side of the tree was Osmond, lying on his back with his arms extended, his head and heels in the mud. His gun was lying over his left arm, and the stock and other parts of it were covered with shot marks. Both barrels of the gun were fully

North Front, Tregothnan. (Authors' collection)

cocked. He had probably been killed by a single shot, which had penetrated his waistcoat and gone through the body.

There was a cap lying nearby; it was correctly assumed that this belonged to the killer. The trail led roughly thirty yards from the body to a little clump of hard bushes, beside which was part of the keeper's watch chain, which was also damaged by the marks of several shots. A close examination of his boots and the two sets of footprints around the bushes suggested that the larger prints were the keeper's, and the smaller ones made by the man presumed to be his assailant.

Police enquiries led them to Dr Bonar, who reported that he had been called earlier in the day to attend to Robert Bullen. Aged forty-three, Bullen had been in the area on the previous afternoon when he was shot near the hip, and had gone back to his cottage to rest in bed. The doctor found a gunshot wound, about 2½in deep, noticed that it contained some dirt and traces of a pheasant's feathers, and cleaned it out.

As if anxious to appease his conscience, Bullen, a dyed-in-the-wool poacher, made no secret of what had happened. While spending the afternoon at Nancemabyn Wood, he told the doctor, 'Someone fired at me, and I, all in a moment, fired back.' He did not know whether he had hit anybody or not.

Later on 26 January Dr Bonar returned to the cottage, told Bullen a man was missing, and that they were searching for him. Bullen immediately said, 'Then I must have struck him; go to the policemen and the searchers in Nancemabyn Wood, and tell them that I did it.' Bonar then went to meet the searchers at the wood, and caught up with them shortly after the body had been found. On 27 January, Dr Cholmeley of Truro made a post-mortem examination and counted between sixty and seventy shot entries around the wound on the chest. Bonar thought the gun must have been fired at a distance of about five yards, and all the pellets came from one charge. There were several shot wounds in the left lung, and in the heart was one wound large enough to admit the little finger.

That same day Dr Bonar visited Bullen again, and found he seemed much better. There was clearly a case to answer, and Bullen was brought to the court in an ambulance. Several witnesses spoke of the movements of both men on the previous day, and of Bullen's confession when the doctor was called in to dress the gunshot wound. The jury returned a verdict of wilful murder against Bullen, who was committed for trial. He was then taken back to his house again to return to bed, but still under arrest.

In the evening, Superintendent Bassett accompanied Dr Bonar to Bullen's house, and found him resting. He formally charged him with killing Osmond, left Sergeant Kendall to keep him under observation, officially in custody, and cautioned him. When the prisoner reiterated that he was shot in Nancemabyn Wood, Bonar said, 'You said you fired back.'

'Yes, he fired at me first, and I fired back at him,' was the answer. 'I don't know whether I struck him or not. I don't know who he was. I heard him say "Oh dear" or "Come here". I don't know which.'

The next day Kendall went to Bullen's former home, now unoccupied, a quarter of a mile away, where he found a recently used double-barrelled breech gun. Bullen admitted it was his. When Kendall told him he could not find any cartridges down there, he said he had no idea where they were. 'Since the house has been under repair, I have had to hide them away, as I found others were using them.'

On 30 January Kendall was present at an interview when Bullen's brother came to the house. Bullen's brother asked him where he had been shot, and Bullen told him. The brother replied, 'The keeper fired high enough too, Bob.' Bullen replied, 'Yes, and for the first few days I wish he had shot me in the head instead; he would have been living to tell the tale then.' When his brother asked how far away the keeper had been when he fired, he replied, 'About seven or eight yards – almost close; he fired at me and I turned and fired at him; it was almost momentary. I did not stop to see if I had struck him.' Bullen had told the doctor that he had lost his cap, and when shown the one by Constable Baker that had been picked up near the dead keeper, he admitted it was his.

On 1 February Kendall told Bullen he intended to return to his old house to search for cartridges. Bullen then told his wife to go to the cupboard in their present house and give him the cartridges in the box.

The case was heard on 21 June at Bodmin Assizes, before Mr Justice Ridley, with Mr McKellar prosecuting. Considerable interest had been aroused by the case, and the courtroom was crowded. Several hundred members of the public were unable to gain admission.

Mr McKellar submitted that Bullen's admission to having fired a shot at a man in the woods, and being subsequently told that it was almost certainly the missing keeper, was undeniable evidence that Osmond was killed by a shot fired by Bullen. This placed the onus on the accused to produce any justification or alleviation in reply to a charge of wilful murder. If what Bullen said was true then he might set up a good defence, but if the excuse he offered did not tally with the whole story, and if it could be proved that part of the statement was actually a lie, the jury would look on it with some hesitation.

Next, the police remarked on finding two sets of footprints close to the body and the marks of Bullen's boots. Nearby was a bush full of shot marks, and a piece of silver chain – part of Osmond's watch and chain. A cap, which Bullen had admitted was his property, was picked up near the body, as was a full cartridge about 6ft away, and an empty one a few feet further than that. Osmond's gun had one barrel empty, and in the other was an empty cartridge. There were gunshot marks on the deceased man's watch, chain, and braces, and a large wound through the heart.

One of the under-gamekeeper's duties was to arrest any man suspected of being a poacher on the estates where he was working. The prosecution submitted that Bullen had fired the first shot at Osmond as the latter passed the wood but it

Mr Justice Ridley. (Authors' collection)

had missed Osmond and hit his gun instead, carried away his watch chain, and entered the bush. Having been shot at and threatened, Osmond intended to arrest Bullen, and fired at him. Bullen was presumably running away, and the under-gamekeeper fired at him to stop him, aiming at the lower part of his body. Then the court had Bullen's admission that, on this shot being fired, he turned and fired, the shot entering Osmond's heart. This, the counsel urged, was a case of wilful murder, the first shot by the accused being evidence of intention.

Osmond's widow confirmed that her husband had left home at about two in the afternoon, taking his dog and gun, to go on duty. At the time there were no shot marks on his gun, watch chain, braces or waistcoat. It was the last time she saw him alive.

Harland Mitchell, a farmer from Tresawle Farm, said he saw Osmond about 6 p.m. on 26 January going towards Nancemabyn Wood, walking quite fast, carrying his gun under his left arm. Ten minutes later he heard two gunshots in quick succession, both from the direction of the wood. This was corroborated by William Carbis, a farm labourer who lived half a mile from the wood.

John Dew, Lord Falmouth's head keeper, said Osmond had been one of his two under-gamekeepers. Dew had joined Constable Baker and others in the search for his body on 27 January. Frederick Stevens, an under-keeper to Lord Falmouth, and Frederick Dunn, keeper to Sir Lewis Molesworth, corroborated.

Superintendent Bassett confirmed that he had charged Bullen on 27 January with killing Osmond.

Frederick Tims, a gunsmith of Cathedral Lane, Truro, stated that he had not seen Bullen in his shop, although Bullen owned cartridges which had been bought from the premises. The shot that removed the chain must have been fired from six to eight yards away. After this, Dr Bonar reported having seen to Bullen's injuries, and quoted the confessions he had made.

This ended the case for the prosecution. On oath, Bullen said that at the time he was living with his wife at Probus, and had not been married long. He had collected his gun on the evening of Tuesday 26 January, had both barrels loaded, saw a pheasant and fired from the right barrel. When the dead bird fell from the sky, he had picked it up and put it in his pocket. He turned to leave the wood and, after going about twelve yards, he was shot in the hip. His immediate fear was that he might have lost his leg. As he turned round, he saw a man standing with a gun.

'He shot me first; I do not know what he fired for. After I fired I heard him say "Oh dear" or "Come here".'

When he fired at the man, he emphasised, he had no intention of killing him. He dropped his cap, but did not stop to retrieve it, then took the gun to the unoccupied house and went home. He had only fired two shots in the wood, one at the pheasant and the other after he had been fired at; he denied firing twice at the keeper.

When cross-examined, he said he had fired five shots altogether after five o'clock, but could not say whether the person who had shot him was the same man who had called out to him. On hearing the call, he had run away. He did not know whether the man was a keeper, could not see whether he had a gun or not, and did not call back again as his sole intention was to keep out of the way and get back home. As he admitted to taking home four pheasants that day, he had every reason to try and remain as inconspicuous as possible. The keeper, he went on, did not speak to him any more than that, and at no point did he see anybody lying on the ground. Nor did he see the keeper fall, aim directly at the deceased, put the pheasants into the keeper's pocket, or touch the keeper's gun after he had been shot. He insisted that he did not fire at the keeper after the latter spoke to him, and he could not say how the bush got marked.

The counsel for the prosecution asked how the one shot could have marked the gun and entered the deceased's heart. Bullen replied that the gun was held in a sideways direction, and he did not go back because he was wounded. The doctor told him that if the shot had turned to the right, instead of going down his thigh, he would never have left the wood alive.

Here the judge said he did not feel satisfied that there ought to be a verdict on the murder charge. It seemed beyond doubt that there were three shots, the first and third having been fired by the prisoner, and the second by the keeper. As there was an element of provocation on the part of the deceased, it was not murder. Either Bullen was guilty of manslaughter or, if the defence could make out an adequate case, he might be acquitted.

Mr Randolph then spoke for the defence. He had nothing more to add, except to confirm the judge's statement that the first shot in the wood had been Bullen firing at a pheasant, the second was the shot fired by the deceased keeper, and the third was the fatal shot fired by Bullen.

In summing up for the jury, the judge said that counsel claimed Bullen had always told the same story, but this was not the case. Not until that day had he explained that the first shot was fired not at Osmond, but at a pheasant in the wood. It was vital that Bullen should explain that first shot if he was going to substantiate his defence in court; it was not possible to say that the third shot was fired in self-defence, as it was inconsistent with the first shot that showed the prisoner wished to attack the under-gamekeeper. Bullen had tried to excuse his actions by saying that it was a case of self-defence, but part of the story had never been told until that day.

After retiring for only a few minutes, the jury returned a verdict that Bullen was guilty of manslaughter. The foreman said that they fully concurred that the prisoner fired the first shot at the under-gamekeeper, the second was fired by the under-gamekeeper, and the third shot was the fatal one fired by the prisoner.

The judge had no hesitation in accepting this verdict. Addressing the prisoner, he said he had told the truth up to a certain point, but not about the first shot. This made a great deal of difference to the case, for if he had merely been fired upon without provocation by the under-gamekeeper, and had then fired back at Osmond, he (the judge) would not have taken such a serious view of it. Nonetheless, he was aware that Bullen had already appeared on nine previous occasions before the magistrates for game trespass and other offences, one of which had resulted in a six-week sentence at Bodmin Assizes for assaulting a keeper. He was obviously not afraid to use violence if it suited him.

'You are an old poacher,' he concluded, 'that is your character; it is no worse than that, but on this occasion you killed a man. You used a deadly weapon, although I don't suggest you have done that before. You will be sentenced to ten years' penal servitude.'

As he was led back to the cells, Bullen's sentence would prove shorter than anybody had imagined. Led away to captivity after the close of court proceedings, he spent three nights at Bodmin Gaol.

Shortly after six o'clock on the morning of 24 June, Assistant Warder Samuel Chapman was doing the rounds of the cells when he found an obstruction against Bullen's door. As he pushed it away, he found the prisoner's body suspended from the ventilator over the door by a piece of string. The body was still warm and artificial respiration was attempted, pending the arrival of a doctor a few minutes later, but by then Bullen was pronounced dead. Since beginning his sentence he had been making sacks, for which plenty of string but no tools were required. At the end of each day the work and spare pieces of string were tidied away and collected by the prison authorities, but it was not the custom to search prisoners' clothing unless they were engaged in outdoor work. Bullen had evidently secreted enough string away to ensure his time there would not be long. An inquest on 25 June returned a verdict that he had 'feloniously killed himself, being then of sound mind'.

24

'LORD HAVE MERCY ON A MISERABLE SINNER'

Gwennap, 1909

Sarah Elizabeth Visick was a pretty young woman, although her good looks and easy virtue had evidently got her into trouble more than once as, by 1909, the twenty-three-year-old domestic servant had given birth to three illegitimate children. The last, a girl named Olive Irene, was put out to nurse with a Mrs Wright shortly after her birth but, on 8 April 1909, Sarah appeared unexpectedly at Mrs Wright's door at six o'clock in the evening and announced that she was taking her baby to another woman, Mrs Johns. Several people saw Sarah walking near Gwennap that evening with the baby wrapped in a shawl but, sadly, the six-and-a-half-week-old infant never arrived at the home of her new nurse.

When asked about her daughter, Sarah gave conflicting accounts of the child's whereabouts, telling some people that she was in the care of a new wet nurse and telling others that a friend had taken the baby to America. When the body of a baby girl was found some weeks later at the bottom of a disused engine shaft at the Wheal St Aubyn mine in Gwennap, the police were soon informed that Sarah's baby daughter had not been seen for quite a while.

Sarah, when interviewed, was unable to tell the police where her baby was. Eventually, she admitted throwing the child down the mineshaft, telling the constable that she had been homeless and destitute at the time and could not afford to pay for the child's upkeep. She asked the constable whether he thought she would be hanged for murder.

That was a question that could only be decided at the Assizes and, on 23 June 1909, Sarah was placed on trial at Bodmin before Mr Justice Phillimore, charged with the wilful murder of her daughter. The prosecutors were Mr O'Connor MP and Mr Stafford Howard, while Sarah was defended by Mr F.C. Jenkin.

Almost immediately after Mr O'Connor opened the case for the prosecution, Sarah Visick slumped to the ground in a faint and had to be carried out of the courtroom and revived. She was to faint several times during the remainder of the proceedings and the local newspaper observed that she was 'evidently in mental agony'.

In spite of her earlier admission to the police, Sarah now pleaded 'Not Guilty' to the charge of wilful murder against her. Testifying under oath, she told the court that, having removed Olive from Mrs Wright's home, she took her for a walk. Sarah stated that she suffered from fits and, while walking with her daughter, she had felt the familiar pains that were always a precursor to her seizures. She had lost consciousness for some time and, when she came round, she checked her baby, finding the little girl motionless and cold. Thinking that she may have accidentally injured the infant while in the throes of her fit, she had tried to revive her, but without success. (Part of the resuscitation process she described to the court was attempting unsuccessfully to put the child's feet in its mouth!)

Mr Justice Phillimore.
(Authors' collection)

125

When Sarah couldn't revive her daughter she panicked and, in fear of being arrested for killing her baby, she decided to hide the child's body in a place where she believed nobody would ever find it. She had thrown the child down the shaft and made up her mind to 'try and keep a cheerful countenance', so that people wouldn't suspect that her baby was dead and accuse her of its murder.

'Before you threw the baby down the shaft, you really thought it was dead?' asked the judge.

'Yes, sir,' replied Sarah.

Much of the case against Sarah Visick hinged on the medical evidence of the doctors who had conducted a post-mortem examination on the body of the dead baby. They had found that the baby had a fractured skull and, having cited this as the cause of the infant's death, told the court that it was their opinion that the baby had been alive when it was thrown down the shaft. However, in cross-examination by the counsel for the defence, the doctors admitted it was possible that the skull fracture had been sustained in the fall after the child had died and that deterioration of the baby's lungs, due to prolonged immersion in the water at the bottom of the mine, might have masked any signs that the child had actually died from suffocation.

Sarah admitted that she had eaten nothing at all on the day of her baby's death and had consequently felt very weak and dizzy. It was possible, she said, that she might have accidentally dropped the baby on the ground in her dizziness and so fractured the child's skull.

The prosecution maintained that Sarah's daughter had been an unwanted baby and that Sarah had deliberately thrown her down the mineshaft to get rid of her. The defence argued that Sarah had accidentally suffocated her daughter whilst having a fit and then disposed of the child's body through fear of accusations. However, the prosecution called the prison doctor as a witness, who testified that, while in custody, Sarah had shown no signs of having epilepsy and, although she had fainted a few times, she had never once fully lost consciousness as a result of her fainting fits.

It was left to Mr Justice Phillimore to sum up the case for the jury, which he did in a most controversial fashion. Rather than confining his remarks to a summary of the evidence, Phillimore intimated to the jury that, if they found Sarah guilty of the wilful murder of her baby, then the death sentence would be passed but she would not be hanged. He added that he was not sure if it was wise for him to publicise such a fact, but he trusted that there was nobody there in court who would be wicked enough to make use of it. Saying that he recognised the jury had a very painful duty to discharge, he told them that the destruction of illegitimate children by mothers was by no means uncommon and there obviously had to be a law in force against such a practice. Yet, for some years, the Home Office policy had been not to hang mothers who killed their children at such a tender age as this and thus Sarah's death sentence would doubtless be commuted to one of penal servitude. She would remain incarcerated until the Home Secretary felt that she had paid her debt to society.

The judge reminded the jury that Sarah had now given birth to three illegitimate children, asking them if, for the good of society, it would be worth considering whether it was better that she should be 'shut up' for a time. Phillimore stressed that he was not trying to influence the jury to find Sarah guilty if they believed that she was innocent. He simply wanted to relieve their minds, knowing that deciding on the capital case of such a young and good-looking girl would be a difficult job for them.

The jury retired for a few minutes, returning with a verdict of 'Guilty of wilful murder', although they tempered their decision with a recommendation for mercy. Sarah swooned again and, having been revived, was asked if she had anything to say. 'I am certain I never intentionally killed my child. I am quite prepared to say that,' she insisted.

Mr Phillimore put on his black cap, at which Sarah went into hysterics. 'Lord have mercy on a miserable sinner!' she shrieked, before swooning again as the judge intoned the death sentence.

'As I told the jury, you will not be hung,' Phillimore reassured her, but Sarah obviously didn't hear his words of intended comfort. Terror etched on her face, she was taken from the court, evidently believing that she was going to die.

Her defence counsel announced that he proposed to appeal the verdict and the case was heard about three weeks later before the Lord Chief Justice, Mr Justice Darling and Mr Justice Jelf at the Court of Criminal Appeal. There, Mr Jenkin accused Mr Justice Phillimore of leading the jury in his summary of the case, giving them the impression that returning a guilty verdict would be in the public interest, in view of the fact that this was the defendant's third illegitimate child.

Having listened to Jenkin's arguments, the three judges refused Sarah Visick leave to appeal her conviction, saying that while they did not endorse the observations made by Phillimore in his summing up, in their opinion, the summary had been fair. They said the jury had been given ample opportunity to consider the defence that the child had died accidentally while her mother was insensible. Sarah Visick herself had told the constable that she had done away with her baby, as she had no home and nowhere to take it. Any reasonable jury ought to have found a guilty verdict; it was unlikely that they had arrived at their decision with the sole aim of preventing a continuation of the defendant's immoral behaviour in producing illegitimate children.

Although Sarah Visick was refused leave to appeal, Mr Justice Phillimore proved correct in his insistence that she would not hang for her crime and, as he had suggested it would be, her sentence was later commuted to one of penal servitude.

Interestingly, another charge of child murder was tried at the same Assizes. This time, the defendant was Louisa Hodge of Altarnun, who was also a domestic servant. Louisa was the daughter of illiterate farm labourers and was described as 'a person of somewhat low intelligence and education'.

One of Louisa's duties in her employment was milking the cows and, on 7 March 1909, she had just milked the first one when she gave birth. The baby cried out, startling the cows, and Louisa picked it up and put it on some straw out of harm's way.

Altarnun. (© N. Sly)

Having finished the milking, Louisa took her newborn son into the farm kitchen, where he died shortly afterwards, in spite of the efforts to keep him alive made by her employer's wife, Mrs Sparkes. Dr Hugh Hamilton Serpell was called to the farmhouse and found that the baby had died from suffocation. There was a cut on his face, running from his lip to his cheek and, when Serpell inspected the child's mouth, he found that it was full of dung, straw and oat husks.

The debris had been tightly packed into the baby's mouth and throat and, in Serpell's opinion, this had been a deliberate act of violence, intended to kill the baby. Louisa Hodge strenuously denied ever having placed anything in her son's mouth, telling the court that she could not explain how the stuff had got there.

In his summary for the jury, Mr Justice Phillimore made no mention of the likely outcome of a guilty verdict, nor did he comment on the fact that seventeen-year-old Louisa already had a three-year-old illegitimate child. Instead, he simply instructed the jury that, if the defendant had stuffed anything into the infant's mouth in order to suffocate it, she was guilty of murder. If the jury believed the baby's death was accidental and there was no neglect of duty, they should acquit her.

It took the jury just ten minutes of deliberation to find Louisa Hodge 'Not Guilty' of the wilful murder of her son. At this the judge informed them that he did not intend to proceed with a charge of manslaughter on the coroner's warrant and discharged her from court, a free woman.

25

'IT WAS NOT SELF-INFLICTED. I DID IT'

Budock, 1918

On 14 January 1918, twenty-five-year-old Thomas John McCarthey staggered into his parents' home near Budock, blood pouring from a wound in his throat. Naturally his horrified mother, Ada, sent for a doctor and when Dr Leonard Hopper arrived, he found that McCarthey had cut his own throat.

The wound was not a serious one and Dr Hopper inserted five or six stitches. When he questioned McCarthey, the young man told him that he wanted to commit suicide and would have finished the job had he not mislaid the razor he had used to make the incision in his throat. Asked why he should want to kill himself, McCarthey told the doctor and his parents that he had murdered his girlfriend that night because she had given him 'a certain disease'.

The police were called to the house and McCarthey obligingly told them exactly where they might find the body of nineteen-year-old Linda Jane Vine. Sergeant Johns and PC Hugo followed his directions to a lonely spot close to the Budock Beacon where, as McCarthey had promised, they found the body of a young woman stretched across a little-used footpath, her head almost severed from her body. There were no signs that any struggle had taken place in the area and it was evident that Miss Vine's attacker had taken her by surprise and felled her where she now lay. Her throat was cut and she had died almost immediately from massive blood loss. McCarthey's National Insurance card lay on top of her body and his cap was found some forty yards away.

The police went back to McCarthey's home, where the doctor pronounced him well enough to be taken into custody at Falmouth police station. He was charged with wilful murder and remanded in custody.

Miss Vine and McCarthey had been 'keeping company' for some time. Their relationship was expected to lead to eventual marriage and they were described in the contemporary newspapers as being 'on the closest intimacy'. Miss Vine originated from Ponsanooth but, at the time of her death, lodged with a labourer and his wife in Shute Lane, Penryn. She did not work, although she frequently helped her landlady with the housework on an informal basis and, since she earned no money, McCarthey contributed the sum of 8s a week towards her lodgings. Before meeting McCarthey, Miss Vine had been expecting to marry a soldier at St Gluvias Church but, although the banns were called in April 1917, her fiancé had failed to put in an appearance for the wedding.

McCarthey formerly worked as a rope maker on The Quay at Penryn. Known as a somewhat shy, retiring young man, he joined the Duke of Cornwall's Light Infantry at the age of eighteen and served for three years, before being discharged due to a defect in his hearing. During his time in the army, McCarthey had seen action in France at the height of the First World War and had been gassed in the trenches. Since returning to Cornwall, he had frequently complained of suffering from severe headaches.

An inquest was opened by coroner Mr E.L. Carlyon. The coroner began by describing the relationship between McCarthey and Miss Vine, telling the jury that McCarthey had suspected his girlfriend was seeing other men, which had caused friction between them. There was no doubt that the girl was murdered by someone, said Carlyon, and it would be the jury's task to determine by whom.

Penryn, where the victim lodged. (Authors' collection)

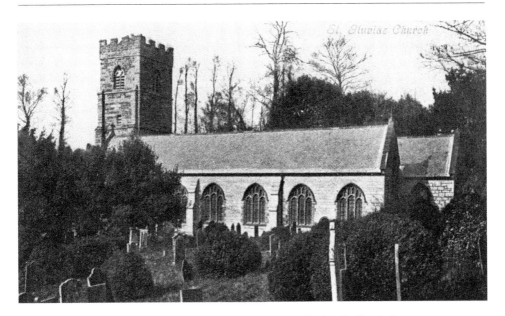

St Gluvias Church, where Miss Vine was expecting to marry. (Authors' collection)

The first witness to testify was the victim's landlord, Alfred Searle. Searle stated that he had known Miss Vine for about four years and had always considered her to be a nice, well-conducted girl. After the death of her parents, she had initially lodged with her sister but then asked the Searles if she could move in with them. At that time, she had been in service but had lost her job, after which she had been unable to pay rent. Searle told the inquest that, for the previous two months, McCarthey had paid for his girlfriend's lodgings.

Searle also stated that, on occasion, Miss Vine would go out at night and return with money, although he had not considered it his business to question her on how she procured it. Since meeting McCarthey, she had not brought home any money.

McCarthey and Linda Vine frequently took walks together and were a familiar sight in the area. Two local policemen told the inquest that they had often seen the couple out and about and, since Miss Vine had met McCarthey, they had not seen her in the company of any other men. PC Dempster had actually seen the couple heading towards the Beacon on the night of the murder and stated that their behaviour was completely normal and they appeared to be on friendly terms.

Mrs Ada McCarthey spoke of her son's return on 14 January. She had been upstairs when he arrived home and called out 'Mother'. When she went downstairs, she saw that his hands were covered in blood and that he was bleeding from a wound in his throat. He had told his mother to fetch a policeman and she had called Dr Hopper.

One of the jurors asked her if there was any history of insanity in the family, but the question was quashed by the coroner before Mrs McCarthey could answer. Mr Carlyon reminded the jury that it was nothing to do with their verdict and would be dealt with in due course, if the accused was committed for trial.

Sergeant Johns was then asked to detail McCarthey's arrest. Johns told the inquest that he had arrived at McCarthey's home and found him lying on the floor, his throat cut. McCarthey told the sergeant, 'I have done in a girl up Beacon. I killed her with a razor. She gave me what I didn't want and I gave she what she didn't want. I tried to do myself in but lost the razor.' Having accompanied PC Hugo to the Beacon and found the body, Johns then returned to McCarthey's home and arrested him, telling him that he would be charged with wilful murder. 'Of course,' responded McCarthey. When McCarthey was searched, a bloodstained razor was found in the lining of his coat.

Dr Hopper testified about his treatment of McCarthey and also about the post-mortem examination he had subsequently conducted on Linda Vine. The doctor confirmed that there were no bruises or marks of violence on the body but Miss Vine had been almost decapitated by the injury to her throat, which had severed her windpipe and all of the main blood vessels. Reports in the contemporary local newspapers neither confirmed nor denied that either Miss Vine or Thomas McCarthey were suffering from 'a certain disease', although the national newspapers stated that the medical evidence showed both were suffering from 'a complaint', which was presumably a venereal disease.

Once the medical evidence was concluded, the coroner summed up the evidence for the jury, telling them that they needed to consider whether the wound on Miss Vine's throat was self-inflicted.

'It was not self-inflicted. I did it,' observed McCarthey.

The jury's verdict of wilful murder against Thomas McCarthey was thus hardly surprising and he was committed to stand trial at the next Assizes on the coroner's warrant.

McCarthey seemed nonchalant about his fate. He appeared before Mr Justice Avory at Bodmin on 28 January 1918, looking pale and unwell, his throat still bandaged. The case was prosecuted by Mr R.E. Dummett, with Mr F.E. Wiltshire representing McCarthey, who almost reluctantly pleaded 'Not Guilty' to the charge against him.

Not unexpectedly, since there were only a few days between the two proceedings, much of the evidence given at the trial was a repeat of that put forward at the inquest. However, as promised by the coroner, the question of McCarthey's sanity at the time of the murder was given full consideration.

Now Mrs Ada McCarthey was allowed to state that her husband had twice been confined in a lunatic asylum, laying the foundations for a defence of hereditary insanity. Much was made by the defence of the fact that McCarthey had been gassed during the war. However, when Dr Hopper was called to give evidence, he stated that, in his opinion, a man's mind would not necessarily be affected by gassing. If he was insane at all, it was more likely to be hereditary insanity, stated Hopper, although he added that he had not formed any opinion on the state of McCarthey's mind in the immediate aftermath of the murder, nor had he personally dealt with any cases of gassing.

Dr Hopper revealed that McCarthey had visited his surgery prior to the murder, at which point he was 'distressed', although at the time he gave Hopper no reason to suspect insanity. (Although it is not specifically stated, it seems reasonable to assume that McCarthey consulted the doctor with the symptoms of a venereal disease.)

Defence counsel Mr Wiltshire stressed to the jury that Miss Vine's murder was not premeditated. Indeed, McCarthey had left a note at home before going out on the night of 14 January that indicated he was going to 'do away with himself'. Any man who attempts suicide is in an unsound state of mind, Wiltshire told the court, adding that in McCarthey's case there was a strong taint of familial insanity on his father's side. Not only that but he had also gone through all the horrors of active combat, in itself sufficient to induce latent lunacy. Wiltshire concluded his speech by stating that he believed there was sufficient evidence for the jury to find that the accused was of unsound mind at the time of the murder.

In his summing up, Mr Justice Avory reminded the jury that, in the eyes of the law, a man was assumed to be sane unless it could be proved otherwise. Thus it was the duty of the jury to determine whether they believed that there was anything in the evidence to justify the conclusion that, at the time of the offence, the accused did not know that he was doing 'a wrong thing'. Avory took issue with Mr Wiltshire's statement that an attempted suicide was the act of a person with an unsound mind, stating that it could just as easily be a coward's way of escaping the responsibility for his own act.

With that, the jury retired, spending seventy minutes deliberating the case before returning a verdict of 'Guilty' against Thomas McCarthey. However, they tempered their verdict with a recommendation of mercy for the prisoner, which Mr Justice Avory promised to bring to the attention of the proper authorities.

Shortly before his execution was scheduled to take place, it was announced that McCarthey's sentence had been commuted to one of life imprisonment.

Note: In the earlier contemporary accounts of the case, McCarthey's name is alternatively given as McCartney. The prosecuting counsel is named as both Mr Dummett and Mr Drummett.

26

'THE WHOLE THING IS THE WORK OF A MANIAC?'

Nanstallon, near Bodmin, 1922

Thursday, 15 June 1922 was a gloriously hot, sunny day and Mr and Mrs Parkin of Pendewey Farm, Nanstallon, rose early with the intention of visiting the annual Royal Cornwall Show at Newquay. Their nine-year-old daughter, Edith Mary, was to attend school as normal and her aunt, Edith Juleff, watched her set off for the one-mile walk at about 8.45 a.m.

Miss Juleff was expecting her niece home for lunch and was surprised and concerned when lunchtime came and went with no sign of the little girl. She sent Edith's older brother, Gordon, to the school to look for his sister and was horrified to learn that Edith had never arrived there that morning. Edith's uncle, Charles Juleff, had planned to go into Bodmin that afternoon and Miss Juleff asked him to look out for Edith there. Meanwhile, Miss Juleff, her brother Wesley and Gordon began an immediate search of the area between the school at Nanstallon and Pendewey Farm. But as the afternoon wore on, and there was still no sign of the missing schoolgirl, Gordon was sent into Bodmin to report her disappearance to the police.

Sergeant Brooking and PC Morcumb conducted their own quick search, sending to Bodmin for reinforcements when they were unable to find Edith. By early evening, the police had organised a large search party, which included many local residents as well as members of the St Petroc Boy Scout Troop and labourers from the nearby railway.

At just after eight o'clock that night, Joseph Sweet, a ganger on the London and South West Railway, found the little girl's body lying face down on the edge of a pit

Above & left:
Nanstallon.
(© N. Sly)

The school, Nanstallon.
(© N. Sly)

in a small plantation, about half a mile from her home and roughly eighty yards off her normal route to school. Her arms were folded over her chest, obviously carefully placed there by whoever had killed her. By chance, Dr A.G. Salmon, the Parkins' family doctor, was visiting a patient at a cottage just a few yards away. Salmon examined Edith, together with police surgeon Dr Charles Hugo, and they noted that the child had a large, deep wound on the back of her head. The body was moved to the East Cornwall Hospital at Bodmin, where it was later determined that Edith had been hit hard on the back of her head with a blunt instrument, fracturing her skull and causing her almost instantaneous death. Her right ear was both bruised and discoloured and she had more bruises and abrasions on her face. *Rigor mortis* had set in and the doctors estimated that Edith had been killed between eight and twelve hours before her body was found.

Although her clothing was disarranged, there was no medical evidence to suggest that she had been sexually assaulted. The contemporary local newspaper reported cryptically, 'One article of clothing was removed but not taken away.'

Within two hours of the discovery of Edith's body, the police had arrested a suspect. Twenty-seven-year-old Charles Juleff was charged with the wilful murder of Edith Mary Parkin the following afternoon and appeared before magistrates at a special sitting, where he was remanded in custody to allow the police time to make further enquiries. Meanwhile, an inquest was opened into Edith's death at the Bodmin Guildhall by the coroner for the Bodmin district, Mr Edyvean. Juleff was transported to the inquest by bus and was forced to take a flying leap from the bus through the doors of the Guildhall to avoid a crowd of hostile people, mainly

The old hospital, Bodmin. (© N. Sly)

women, who booed, hissed and shouted as the bus arrived. The inquest dealt only with evidence of identity before being adjourned.

Charles Juleff was the adopted son of Mrs Parkin's brother, Joseph Juleff, who owned Pendewey Farm. Joseph had worked for many years as an engineer in the mining industry in South America, where he had made a considerable fortune. When he returned to England and purchased a farm near Truro, he brought Charles back with him. Charles was educated at Truro College (now known as Truro School) and managed a fruit farm on leaving. During the First World War, he joined the army and served for four years, seeing action in France. On his discharge, he was apprenticed to a firm of engineers in Lincoln but soon found that he preferred farming to engineering. He had been staying with the Parkins since August 1921 and helped out with casual labour on the farm.

When the inquest into Edith's death was resumed on 28 June, it was revealed that several items of clothing had been sent to Home Office Analyst Mr J. Webster. These included a pair of knickers – presumably the item of Edith's clothing removed but left at the scene – and the grey flannel trousers, grey jacket, string vest, and black boots worn by Charles Juleff on the day of the murder, along with two of his white shirts. Although Mr Webster did not appear at the inquest in person, his report was read out and it stated that a single spot of blood had been found on the knickers, along with three spots of blood on Juleff's jacket. No blood had been found on any of Juleff's other clothes and, at the time of Edith's disappearance, he was known to have an existing cut on his nose, caused when he had tripped over a chair and hit his face on a rocking horse. Juleff had willingly submitted to a thorough medical examination by Dr Hugo on the night of his arrest and, apart from bruising and the scab on his nose, had no marks or blood anywhere on his body.

Following Mr Webster's report, the inquest heard from Edith's father, John Parkin, who stated that there had been no quarrel between Juleff and Edith. Parkin confirmed that Juleff had cut his face some time before the murder and had been wearing his grey jacket at the time. Parkin told the inquest that he had always considered Charles Juleff to be a quiet, steady man.

Parkin also revealed that an inmate from the Bodmin Asylum had shown a lot of interest in Edith in the weeks before her death. Inmate Arthur Lobb was what was known as 'a patient on parole' and was thus allowed enough freedom to work on the asylum farm. By being outside the confines of the asylum, he had broken his terms of parole, but, according to John Parkin, Lobb had often called at Pendewey Farm, where he was usually given a cup of tea. On several occasions, Lobb had given Edith bunches of flowers and, although he did not regard Lobb as dangerous in any way, John Parkin told the inquest that he had been concerned that he was getting too friendly with his daughter.

The next witness to testify at the inquest was Edith's aunt, Edith Juleff. Miss Juleff confirmed that the clothes sent to Mr Webster for analysis were those worn by Charles Juleff on the day of the murder. She was then questioned about the events of the morning of 15 June. Having told the inquest that her niece left home at 8.45 a.m.,

Miss Juleff went on to recount Charles's movements at around that time. Bizarrely, although Miss Juleff could recall in great detail what Charles had done after Edith left for school, she claimed to have little recollection of what happened in the house before the child left. In addition, the evidence Miss Juleff gave at the inquest differed from that which she had given in her original statement to the police.

Penzance solicitor Mr J. Vivian Thomas, who was attending the inquest on behalf of the Public Prosecutor, quizzed Miss Juleff at great length to try and get a true picture of the day in question. She told the inquest that Charles had eaten his breakfast at eight o'clock then, just before Edith left for school, he had taken milk to some kittens in a barn on the farm. This had taken him about three minutes and he had returned to the farmhouse just as Edith was leaving. He had then gone to feed the hens and collect the eggs, returning to the farmhouse at between 9.15 and 9.30 a.m., after which he had fetched some water for Miss Juleff. He stained some wood for a bookcase he was making and, at some stage during the morning, had picked some shallots from the farm's kitchen garden. Later that day he had changed into his good clothes to go into Bodmin, when she had asked him to keep a look out for Edith, who had not returned for lunch.

Whereas Miss Juleff was quite specific about the timing of Charles's movements after Edith left the house, she claimed not to know what he did between finishing his breakfast and feeding the kittens, leaving between thirty to forty-five minutes unaccounted for. Because Miss Juleff was so vague about this missing time, it cast doubts on the precision of her recall of events after Edith left the house. In addition, in her original statements to the police, she had told Inspector Basher that Charles had fed the poultry, collected the eggs and fetched the water before Edith left for school. Faced with difficult questions from the solicitor for the Crown, Miss Juleff claimed to have been so frightened at finding her niece missing that she may have become confused when talking to the police, but now that she had time to think, she was confident that her testimony was accurate.

Miss Juleff had also told the police that, before her niece left home, Charles had said something to her, which she now denied having ever said. Mr Vivian Thomas told the inquest that, after giving her original statement to the police, she had later asked if she might correct some of the information she had provided and gave a revised statement on 19 June. Mr Vivian Thomas intimated that this had occurred after a chance meeting between Miss Juleff and Mr Webber, a clerk who worked for Mr Elliot Square – the solicitor acting in the interests of Charles Juleff at the inquest. Miss Juleff admitted that she had met a man from Plymouth, who had told her that she need not say anything to the police unless she wished to. She also admitted to talking to Mr Webber, but maintained that she had been questioned by dozens of people since the murder. 'I never saw him alone,' she insisted, at which Mr Vivian Thomas assured her that he was not suggesting anything improper had occurred. Mr Square refuted any suggestion that his clerk had advised Miss Juleff on her evidence and eventually she was dismissed. The inquest jury was later to comment that they were far from satisfied by the evidence given by both Mr Parkin and by Miss Juleff.

The inquest then heard from other witnesses who had been in the area at the time of Edith Parkin's disappearance. Gordon Parkin had seen Charles Juleff eating his breakfast at eight o'clock then had not seen him again until lunchtime. Although he had not mentioned the fact to the police, Gordon now recalled that Charles had asked him for a hammer at lunchtime. Gordon added that he had frequently seen inmates from the Bodmin Asylum, including Arthur Lobb, close to the area where his sister's body was later found.

The postman had delivered a parcel to Pendewey Farm a few minutes before nine o'clock in the morning but had seen neither young Edith nor Charles Juleff. Shortly afterwards, he had seen a party of inmates working on the asylum farm, although none had been anywhere near the road.

Dr Rivers, the Assistant Medical Officer from the County Asylum at Bodmin, stated that Arthur Lobb had been painting the inside of his hut on the morning of the murder between 8.50 and 9.15 a.m. and had later worked on the farm. His presence there was confirmed by attendants William Baker and George Sleeman.

Dr Hugo was then asked to summarise the medical evidence. Having catalogued Edith's injuries, he was of the opinion that she had been felled by a single fatal blow to the back of her head. Mr Square complained bitterly that, although he had applied to the police for a copy of the medical evidence, it had not been forthcoming, making any cross-examination of Dr Hugo a near impossibility. Square asked the coroner if information that may be of use to the defence was being deliberately withheld.

For Mr Square's benefit, Dr Hugo went over the medical evidence in great detail.

'The whole thing is the work of a maniac?' asked Mr Square.

'I should say it was a very extraordinary act,' agreed Dr Hugo.

'All killing is the act of a maniac or of a very strong-willed person,' interjected the coroner, after which Dr Salmon was called to corroborate Dr Hugo's testimony.

Members of the local police force were then asked about the search for Edith, the finding of her body and the subsequent arrest of Charles Juleff on suspicion of her murder.

'What was the suspicion against Juleff?' Mr Square asked Sergeant Brooking, who replied that Juleff's demeanour on the day of the murder had aroused suspicion, along with interviews with Edith's aunt, Miss Juleff. Brooking told the inquest that he had been present at the farm when Juleff returned from his trip to Bodmin, at which time it was suggested that the farm's orchard was searched. According to Brooking, Juleff responded, 'That's no good.'

'What is any good? Can you tell where she is?' someone asked him.

'Off on the fling, I suppose,' replied Juleff casually. He then turned to some of the men present at the farm and suggested that they went to look down the road. In her first interview with the police in the immediate aftermath of the murder, Miss Juleff had told them that Charles and Edith left the house at the same time, although she was later to change her statement.

Inspector Basher recalled interviewing Charles Juleff at the farm and taking a statement from him at the time. In his statement, Charles said that he had got up between 7 and 7.30 a.m. and eaten breakfast with Edith. He then fed the kittens and, by the time he returned, Edith had left for school. Charles recalled feeding the chickens and collecting the eggs, then working on a bookcase he was making until lunchtime. When Edith hadn't come home for lunch, he had gone to Bodmin, returning to help with the search.

However, Mrs Jane Hambly, who lived on the Nanstallon to Bodmin road, was convinced that she had seen Charles walking towards Bodmin on the day of the murder at between 11 and 11.30 a.m., telling the inquest that they had exchanged greetings. This was obviously before lunchtime and was consistent with another witness, Susan Simmons, who claimed to have seen Juleff in Bodmin and asked him if Edith had been found yet.

'I didn't know she was lost,' replied Juleff. However, a second witness, William Robert Southern, had met Juleff in Bodmin later that afternoon and asked him the same question.

'Most likely she will return soon,' Juleff responded.

Inspector Basher told the inquest that, when he asked Charles Juleff to accompany him to Bodmin police station for questioning, Juleff became agitated, saying 'My Christ, My Christ'. Yet even though the police believed that Juleff's demeanour was unusual, not one of the other witnesses had noticed even the slightest abnormality in his behaviour on the day of the murder.

Once the coroner had summed up the evidence for his jury, they retired for only a few minutes before returning with their verdict. They were in full agreement that Edith Mary Parkin had been murdered by fracture of her skull but attributed the murder to person or persons unknown.

Charles Juleff made his fourth appearance before magistrates at Bodmin police station, much to the disappointment of the crowds who gathered outside the Assize Hall anticipating a lengthy trial. The proceedings lasted less than two minutes, as Mayor Mr C.J. Stephens was advised that the police were offering no evidence against Juleff and the case against him was dismissed. By order of the Director of Public Prosecutions, Deputy Chief Constable Superintendent Banfield instructed the mayor to formally discharge Charles Juleff, who walked from the police station minutes later a free man.

Juleff maintained that he had always known he would be freed, adding that he had been very well treated by the police. 'It has all been a load of rot,' was his final comment to reporters as he was driven back to Pendewey Farm by Joseph Juleff.

Nobody else was ever charged with the murder of Edith Parkin and, at the time of writing, the case remains unsolved.

27

'I WOULD GIVE ALL I POSSESS IF I COULD ONLY HAVE HER BACK'

St Breward, 1924

Roger and Owen Hawken left the village of St Breward on the evening of 5 September 1924 for a trip to the Wembley Exhibition in London, organised for employees of the English China Clay Company. The two men lived with their parents and younger brother, Joseph, at Key Bridge, where their father, Richard, owned a farm. For the previous nine weeks, the boys had also shared the house with their married sister, Gladys, and her two young children.

Gladys was married to Horace Russell Hill, a stonemason from St Breward. Although the marriage was happy, the couple had recently fallen on hard times since Horace was on strike. Gladys and the children had been forced to move from their home in St Breward to her parents' home and, unfortunately, there just wasn't enough room for Horace too. Hence, Horace moved back to live with his own mother, although he continued to see his wife and daughters regularly and last visited them on the evening of 6 September.

On Sunday 7 September, before her brothers returned from their work outing, Gladys rushed into her father's bedroom. 'Have you been in the boys' room?' she asked him and, when Richard Hawken said that he had not, Gladys informed him that it had been ransacked. While Richard got dressed, Gladys's mother, Annie, went straight to her sons' room, finding that a locked box belonging to Roger had been prised open.

The room was on the first floor and it would have been impossible for anyone to get in from outside without using a ladder. Once dressed, Richard Hawken inspected the window and sills for marks, but found nothing. He then went outside and checked the position of the farm ladders. Only the previous day, he had been using one of them on a hayrick and had returned it to its usual place. It was immediately obvious to Richard that none of the three farm ladders had been moved.

Leaving his wife to deal with the situation, Richard went to fetch his cows in. By the time he got back, Roger and Owen had returned from London. Told that his box had been broken into, Roger ran upstairs to check his belongings and found that a wallet containing nearly £40 was missing.

The police were called and PC Snell and Inspector Crocker questioned everybody there, with the exception of Richard Hawken, who was out working on the farm. Like everyone else, Gladys was questioned and could offer no explanation for the missing money. Once the police had spoken to her, she busied herself preparing and cooking the family's Sunday lunch, while tending to her two daughters, Gwendoline Mary, aged two years and eight months and baby Winifred. At one stage, while she was being questioned by Inspector Crocker, Gladys turned to her brother Roger and asked him incredulously, 'Do you accuse me of such a thing as this?'

'It is in the hands of the police and I cannot say anything about it,' replied Roger. Try as they might, the police were unable to find any evidence that anyone had either broken into the house or entered through the bedroom window and stolen the money. The two police officers eventually left the Hawkens' farm at one o'clock, saying that they would return later that afternoon. As Richard Hawken was later to say, everyone was 'all worried up' and the activities of that morning meant that they ate lunch much later than usual. It was fairly obvious by then that whoever had stolen the money had access to the house and as they sat down to their meal, Roger appealed to the whole family.

'If anyone in the house has got it they had better hand it back and probably nothing will be said.' Nobody admitted knowing the whereabouts of his money.

The family ate their lunch and, although they were all a little unsettled by the morning's events, nobody's behaviour seemed at all suspicious or out of the ordinary. Gladys was occupied with feeding her children and told Mrs Hawken, 'Mother, look in the oven and see that the pudding doesn't burn.'

By two o'clock they had all finished eating and Gladys took the children upstairs. Only a short while later, Owen went upstairs and, although baby Winifred was sleeping peacefully in her cradle, there was no sign of her mother or older sister.

Owen went back downstairs and asked where Gladys and Gwendoline were. Nobody had seen either of them since the family finished their meal and Gladys had not told anybody that she was going out. The family walked round the house calling for her but there was no reply. 'Perhaps she has gone to pick blackberries?' suggested Mrs Hawken.

Everyone went outside to look for Gladys and Gwendoline but they were nowhere to be seen. The family went off in different directions, all calling Gladys's name.

Owen Hawken had a terrible feeling that there was something more to his sister's disappearance than picking blackberries and, when his mother voiced the same suspicion, saying 'Perhaps she has drowned herself?' he headed for the De

Lank River, which flowed close to their home. As soon as he got there, he spotted Gwendoline's body floating in the water.

Owen waded into the river and grabbed his niece, dragging her onto the bank. She was not breathing and Owen tried giving her artificial respiration; when the little girl showed no response to his frantic efforts to revive her, he ran for help. Meeting his younger brother Joseph, he shouted to him to get the police before rousing two neighbours, Mr Nottle and Mr Denis. The three men ran back to Gwendoline and continued trying to bring her back to life.

Meanwhile, Joseph had met up with PC Snell, who was cycling back to the farm to continue his enquiries into the robbery. When Joseph tearfully told him that he believed his sister and niece were in the river, Snell threw his bicycle into the hedge and raced across the meadow.

Gwendoline was lying on the bank, her little body completely cold and unresponsive. PC Snell tried in vain to revive her until Joseph Hawken suddenly shouted that he had spotted his sister's body a little way along the river, trapped by the current against a large rock.

Snell waded into the water to retrieve the body and, once it was safely on the riverbank, he began artificial respiration. Sadly, just like her daughter, Gladys Hill proved impossible to revive.

Dr Arthur Bailey Pugh from St Tudy was summoned to the scene and pronounced life extinct. A later post-mortem examination confirmed that both Gladys and Gwendoline had died from drowning and the doctor theorised that Gladys had simply walked into the water, holding her daughter's hand, and that Gwendoline would probably have struggled before she finally died.

An inquest was opened into the two deaths at the Penpont Institute on 8 September by Bodmin coroner Mr Edyvean. By that time, £27 of the missing money had been found in an attic above a bedroom in the house, although the remaining money

De Lank River, St Breward. (© N. Sly)

and the wallet in which it was contained were still unaccounted for. The police had also found a chisel that corresponded with the marks on Roger's box, where it had been forced open.

The main witnesses at the inquest were members of Gladys Hill's family. Her husband, Horace, had visited her the night before her tragic death. He told the inquest that she had seemed in good spirits and that she had not given him any money at that time.

Gladys's distraught father confirmed that his daughter had behaved perfectly normally in the days prior to her death and although, like the rest of the family, she had been a little 'excited' by the arrival of the police on Sunday morning, she had seemed her normal bright, cheerful self at lunch. 'Poor unfortunate woman.' Her father sobbed. 'I would give all I possess if I could only have her back.'

Richard Hawken confirmed that Gladys's marriage had been happy and that she and Horace had got on 'splendidly'. As far as Richard was aware, his daughter had no real financial worries. Gladys was very fond of her children, especially the 'little dear that she took with her'. She got on well with all her brothers and was particularly close to Roger, the brother whose money had been stolen. While it was not common knowledge in the household that Roger had money stashed away, his father told the inquest that Gladys must have known. There were three locked boxes in the boys' bedroom and Roger's was the only one of the three that had been forced open.

Everyone who testified agreed that Gladys had been in the house until two o'clock on Sunday 7 September and her body was found in the river no more than thirty minutes later. Nobody had entertained even the slightest suspicions of her intentions. She was normally a happy girl and had no history of any mental or physical illness.

PC Snell told the inquest that he had questioned Gladys in relation to the missing money but she had not appeared distressed in any way by his interrogation, although she had seemed a little pensive. Before leaving, he and Inspector Crocker had made it quite clear to the whole family that they believed nobody had entered the house by the window to steal the money from the bedroom. As far as the police were concerned, the theft was an 'inside job' and could only have been perpetrated by somebody within the household.

The implication was that Gladys had stolen the money from her brother and had been so ashamed by her actions, and so fearful of the consequences, that she had drowned herself and her daughter and, after deliberating in private for a few minutes, this was exactly the verdict reached by the coroner's jury. They unanimously agreed that Gladys Hill had murdered Gwendoline Mary and then committed suicide, while in the grip of a temporary insanity.

Note: It seems to have been customary in the Hawken family to refer to the children by their middle names. Hence Gladys is actually named Rosalie Gladys Hill, Roger is William Roger French Hawken and Owen is Thomas Owen Hawken.

28

'SHE WAS BESIDE HERSELF THROUGH DISEASE OF THE MIND'

Pool, 1952

Although she had been married for five years, when Mrs Joyce May Dunstan was admitted to the sanatorium at Tehidy suffering from tuberculosis, she formed what was described in the newspapers of the time as 'an unnatural attachment' with another patient. On her discharge from the sanatorium, Joyce returned to her marital home but stayed there only a few days before deciding that she would prefer to be with her lesbian lover, Bertha Mary Scorse. Joyce and Bertha lived together at Scorse's mother's home in Newlyn for about sixteen months, although their relationship was punctuated by frequent arguments, mainly precipitated by the fact that, while Joyce's health was steadily improving, Bertha's was deteriorating rapidly.

On 12 January 1952, Bertha and Joyce had the latest of their violent quarrels and, two days later, Joyce left, fleeing to her family home in Pool. Bertha immediately announced her intention to get her to come back and, accompanied by her sister Elizabeth and an aunt, she set off in a taxi in pursuit of her lover. When they arrived at her home, Joyce was persuaded to come outside to talk to Bertha. Another argument ensued and, after a brief struggle between the two women, Joyce fell to the ground, stabbed three times. Leaving Joyce bleeding heavily, Bertha urged the taxi driver to drive off quickly before the police were called.

Joyce was rushed to the Camborne and Redruth Hospital where it was found that two of her three stab wounds were superficial. However, the third wound, located at the bottom of her breastbone, had penetrated her body almost to her spine, piercing her liver and pancreas. Unusually for the 1950s, Joyce was given two blood transfusions and, later that day, she faced emergency surgery to try and halt the severe internal bleeding. Although she survived the surgery, Joyce's condition was causing grave concern and her prognosis was poor. Detective Inspector Roberts was naturally keen to interview her and, having been informed that she was likely to die from her injuries, Joyce gave a deposition from her hospital bed, in the presence of a local magistrate. She told Roberts that Bertha had bought a knife at the very beginning of their relationship and had threatened to use it if anyone ever tried to separate them.

Joyce died on 16 January 1952 and Bertha was charged with her wilful murder. Taken to prison, she twice attempted to commit suicide in the run-up to her trial. Her tuberculosis worsened, necessitating the removal of one of her lungs and, by the time her trial opened at the Devon Assizes in Exeter before Mr Justice Pilcher, she was so ill that she was brought into court on a stretcher, where she remained throughout the two-day duration of the proceedings.

The knife that Bertha had used to stab her lover was a sheath knife with a 5in blade and, when recovered, it was found to carry several pink and green wool fibres, matching a vest and jumper worn by the victim. It was also heavily bloodstained, the blood being of the same group as that of Joyce Dunstan, and Bertha Scorse's fingerprints were found on the handle.

Although the forensic evidence against Bertha Scorse was conclusive and her murderous attack on Joyce Dunstan had been witnessed by several people, the counsel for the defence, Mr John Maude QC, first argued that Bertha had simply held out the knife in a 'threatening gesture', trying to force Joyce to come back to her. He suggested that Joyce had accidentally run onto the knife, which had penetrated her body, causing her fatal injuries. Apart from the fact that Joyce had been stabbed three times, pathologist Dr F.D.M. Hocking had conducted a post-mortem examination on her body and found that, as well as the knife wounds, Joyce had other marks of violence on her body. Bruising on the left side of her chest suggested that she had been punched and her right wrist was also bruised, which Hocking believed was an indication that her arm had been tightly gripped – probably when she raised it to defend herself.

Maude then argued that Bertha Scorse was so severely affected by physical and mental illness at the time of the stabbings that she was completely incapable of differentiating between right and wrong. Calling his client 'a dying woman', Maude insisted, 'She was beside herself through disease of the mind.' However, the prosecution counsel, Mr G.D. 'Khaki' Roberts QC, rebutted this argument by calling Dr J.C.M. Matheson, the principal medical officer of Brixton Prison.

Matheson told the court that Bertha had refused to be interviewed by him in Exeter Prison, telling him that she was 'acting on instructions', and while she was undoubtedly very sick physically, he believed that she was sane.

In his summary of the evidence for the jury, Mr Justice Pilcher seemed to endorse the case for the prosecution. Calling the relationship between Bertha and Joyce

Assize court and council offices, Exeter, 1909. (Authors' collection)

'a perverted passion', Pilcher pointed out that when Bertha travelled from Newlyn to Pool, she had just one thought in mind – to persuade Joyce to renew their relationship. Pilcher asked the jury to consider why Bertha had taken the knife with her and what she intended to do with it. Bertha knew that she had done wrong; what the jury must determine was whether there had been a short interval during which 'reason was dethroned' and she had temporarily lost the ability to differentiate between right and wrong.

It took the jury an hour of deliberation to pronounce Bertha Mary Scorse 'Guilty' of the wilful murder of her lover. Mr Justice Pilcher asked for the stretcher on which Bertha had lain throughout the trial to be raised slightly, so that Bertha could face him as he pronounced the death sentence.

However, just days after the trial, the Home Secretary recommended a reprieve. Her sentence was commuted to one of life imprisonment and, in view of Bertha's ill-health it was widely expected to be a short sentence. Yet, far from being the 'dying woman' described by her defence counsel, Bertha went on to spend the next twenty years incarcerated in prisons the length and breadth of the country. A 'life sentence' usually meant a prison sentence of no more than seven or eight years, but by 1972 Bertha had become the then longest serving female prisoner in the country.

Because she had been deemed sane at the time of her trial, she was not sent to a high security hospital for treatment but instead served her time in mainstream prisons. Released on licence in August 1959, she was recalled to prison the following March after getting drunk and using threatening language. Two years later, she was again released but was subsequently recalled a year later after taking drugs.

By 1971, Bertha was attending group therapy at an outside hospital, having been told that this was a condition of any consideration of her release in the future. However, having completed her course of therapy no release date was forthcoming. In the spring of 1972, she was given a part-time job outside the prison and an expected release date of November that year. Even so, her release was conditional on her spending six months living in an after-care hostel.

In the run-up to her release, Bertha returned to Holloway Prison drunk and subsequently assaulted one of the warders. Brought before magistrates, she was given a severe reprimand, her employment was terminated and her release date cancelled. Told that she was to be transferred to Styal Prison, Cheshire, Bertha barricaded herself in her cell in protest – but to no avail.

In an article published on 11 September 1972 in the *Guardian and Observer*, journalist Jill Tweedie theorised that Bertha (now known as Mary) had spent so long incarcerated simply because she was a lesbian. Tweedie wrote, 'Being a lesbian in prison means relationships between prisoners and prison officers that involve emotions, fears and stresses avoided by the heterosexual prisoner.'

However, Tweedie's article also highlighted another conundrum in the case of Bertha Scorse, which was that she had never once been officially diagnosed as suffering from any mental illness. 'Is Mary to continue serving an endless sentence, too unstable for release, too stable for help?' asked Tweedie.

Bertha Mary Scorse is believed to have died in 1995, aged sixty-four. Although it has not proved possible to discover whether or not she died a free woman, the place of her death is recorded as Islington, the location of London's Holloway Prison.

29

'COME QUICK. THERE HAS BEEN AN ACCIDENT'

Newquay, 1958

In seaside towns like Newquay, much of the area's income depends on the tourist trade. Hence Saturdays in the summer are traditionally 'changeover' days, when visitors vacate their hotel rooms and campsites and return home, to make way for the next week's influx of holidaymakers.

Harold Wilfred Hand from Oldham was coming to the end of his holiday. Sixty-five-year-old Harold, a retired milkman, had been staying in a hotel in Pentire Crescent with his wife, daughter and son-in-law, and on Friday, 12 July 1958, the young couple decided to do some last-minute shopping, before returning to Oldham the following morning.

Mrs Hand suffered from a heart condition and Harold himself was quite a frail man, so they elected not to go shopping. While their daughter and son-in-law walked around Newquay, Mr and Mrs Hand were quite content to relax in the car at Towan Headland, admiring the spectacular view and watching the breaking waves.

Just after 11.30 a.m., Mr Hand decided to go for a stroll. He walked eighty yards across the grassy headland to the public toilets and, as his wife watched from the car, he went inside. Only a couple of minutes later, three holidaymakers from the North of England went into the toilets and saw a young man in a green shirt bending over another man, who was lying on the floor, bleeding from his head. The young man told them that the elderly man had fallen down and hurt himself and that he was going to call for an ambulance. He then dashed out of the toilets, running in the

150

direction of the Headland Hotel. One of the three tourists followed him but was soon outpaced by the running man and eventually lost sight of him among the crowds of people out enjoying the summer sunshine.

However, the man in the green shirt apparently kept his word, as a 999 call was logged from a telephone box near the Headland Hotel. The anonymous male told the operator, 'Come quick. There has been an accident,' before giving the location of the emergency and hanging up the telephone without identifying himself.

The police and an ambulance raced to the scene and the injured elderly gentleman was rushed to the Royal Cornwall Infirmary at Truro where, shortly after admission, he was sent to the operating theatre for emergency surgery. Meanwhile, Mrs Hand was becoming ever more concerned by her husband's prolonged absence. When her daughter and son-in-law returned from their shopping trip and noticed the flurry of activity around the nearby public conveniences, they approached the police and identified the injured man from his description as Mr Hand. The family were quickly driven to his bedside at the hospital.

Although Mr Hand's injuries initially appeared to have resulted from a fall, when the ambulance left, one of the witnesses happened to see a ball of crumpled, bloodstained newspaper in a corner of the toilet facility. When he looked more closely, he realised that the newspaper contained a large rock.

Now faced with what appeared to be a vicious and unprovoked attack on an elderly gentleman, the police were aware that the majority of tourists in the vicinity would be leaving the area the next morning to go home. They immediately set up road blocks all around the town and began a search for the man described by the three northern tourists, who was said to be:

Newquay. (Authors' collection)

... approximately twenty-five years of age, 5ft 6in or 5ft 7in tall, with a stocky build, broad shoulders, a round face, fair complexion, dark hair greased and brushed back, wearing a green open-necked shirt with the sleeves rolled up and medium grey flannel trousers.

When Harold Hand died at five o'clock that afternoon, without ever having regained consciousness, the investigations into what was now his murder stepped up a gear. The head of the Cornwall CID, Detective Superintendent Sidney Roberts, was faced with the grim knowledge that almost half of the town would be leaving the next morning, dispersing all over the country, and that every single one of them had to be contacted before they left the area.

Roberts cancelled all police leave and called policemen back from their holidays, drafting every available police officer in the county to Newquay, to help in the search for 'Green Shirt'. The officers began a house-to-house enquiry that was to include every single guesthouse and hotel in the town, delivering batches of questionnaires to be completed by each owner, guest and member of staff.

The questionnaires asked respondents for their name, the name and address of their accommodation, their home address, the names of everyone who was with them on holiday and their whereabouts between 11.30 a.m. and noon on Friday 11 July. It also asked if they had seen anyone matching the description of 'Green Shirt' or if they had seen anybody behaving suspiciously near the public toilets at the relevant time. In all, more than 4,000 hotels, guesthouses and private residences were visited.

While the house-to-house enquiries were taking place, more police officers patrolled the town, calling at beaches, cinemas, theatres and cafés in their search for 'Green Shirt'.

On Saturday morning, the police drove around the streets of Newquay with loudhailers, appealing for anyone who was on or near the Headland at the time of the murder to contact them. Anxious to help the police with their enquiries, members of the public flocked to the police station with information.

A man had been seen hanging around Newquay golf course and a second man was seen apparently trying to conceal himself in the sand dunes between Holywell and Perranporth. The police immediately scrambled a helicopter from RAF St Mawgan and Inspector C.P. Cole was flown over the area, which was now being combed by troops from the Royal Leicesters, along with members of the Civil Defence Organisation. The police boarded all buses and trains leaving the area, and any man who matched the description of 'Green Shirt' was challenged and asked to provide some form of identification. Nobody bearing even the slightest resemblance to 'Green Shirt' escaped the attention of the vigilant officers and several unfortunate look-alikes complained of being stopped and interrogated time and time again.

The police also appealed for assistance in the local newspapers and radio stations, as well as broadcasting announcements at theatres and cinemas, after which uniformed policemen were stationed outside to question patrons as they left the premises.

On Saturday, it was decided to call in Scotland Yard and, early on Sunday morning, Detective Superintendent Jack Marner and Detective Sergeant Jack Stetson arrived in Newquay, along with Mr J. Gliddon from the Bristol Forensic Laboratory.

A post-mortem examination, conducted on Mr Hand by county pathologist Dr F.D.M. Hocking, indicated that he had a large, gaping wound on the back of his head, beneath which his skull was fractured and his brain severely damaged. Hocking believed that the wound had been caused by a blunt object, such as the large rock found in the toilet facility. At least four additional blows had been struck, any of which would have been sufficient to render Mr Hand unconscious.

The police theorised that the motive for the attack on Mr Hand was robbery, although his wallet, still containing £70, was found hanging on a cord around his neck and it was thought that his assailant may have been interrupted by the arrival of the three men at the public convenience. Shortly after his arrival in Newquay, Detective Superintendent Marner announced that several fingerprints had been lifted at the toilets and had been sent to Scotland Yard, along with the rock used as the murder weapon. However, Marner stressed that members of the public were the key to solving the murder and appealed for more people to come forward, whether or not they believed they had seen anything of importance. 'It is just as important that we should meet those who saw nothing as those who might have seen the killer himself,' he insisted.

In the aftermath of Mr Hand's brutal murder, the police interviewed more than 40,000 people, including Newquay residents, hotel owners and staff and around 30,000 holidaymakers. Everyone with a record of violent crime in the area was interviewed and eliminated from the enquiry. Dozens of holidaymakers reported to their local police stations on their arrival home and a plan of the crime scene was sent to every police station in the country, to assist their officers with the questioning of potential witnesses.

In all, only around 150 people who had been on the Headland at the relevant time were traced. The police interviewed every one of them, scrutinising their holiday photographs for clues, but to no avail. Several people were brought in for further questioning, including a young man whose green shirt bore several bloodstains. Initially a strong suspect, the man was eventually released without charge, since Mr Hand had group O blood and the stains on the suspect's shirt were tested as group A.

The police still had not traced the man who had made the anonymous 999 call, nor had they spoken to the man found bending over Mr Hand in the public convenience. 'It may be one and the same person,' stated Superintendent Roberts, renewing his appeal for the man or men to come forward. Indeed, the police were still keen to hear from any member of the public who might have any useful information. 'This could prove the vital link which, together with information we have already received, would complete the chain,' said Roberts who, like the majority of his colleagues, was convinced that the answer to the question of who killed Harold Hand would eventually be found in Newquay.

By the time the inquest into Mr Hand's death was concluded at Truro on 19 December 1958, the missing link had still not been identified and the coroner's jury returned a verdict of 'Murder by someone whose identity is not yet known'.

On 3 July 1959, the body of twenty-eight-year-old Thomas Nicholls, who was employed as a porter at the Headland Hotel, was found with severe head injuries just yards from where Mr Hand was discovered fatally wounded. 'We are not calling it murder at this stage,' stated Sidney Roberts and indeed, just two days later, he was to declare that Nicholls' death was the result of a tragic accidental cliff fall, rather than murder, and was not connected in any way to the death of Harold Hand.

Despite spawning what was, at the time, the biggest ever man-hunt in Cornwall, the murder of Harold Hand, which became known as 'The Green Shirt Murder', was never solved.

Note: Initial reports of the murder in the local and national newspapers give the victim's name as Horace Hand or Hands. Detective Superintendent Roberts is referred to as both Sidney and Sydney.

BIBLIOGRAPHY

NEWSPAPERS

Birmingham Daily Post
Daily News
Freeman's Journal & Daily Commercial Advertiser
Guardian
Guardian and Observer
Hull Packet
Ipswich Journal
Leeds Mercury
Lloyd's Weekly Newspaper
Manchester Guardian
Morning Chronicle
Reynolds's Newspaper
Royal Cornwall Gazette
The Times
Trewman's Exeter Flying Post or Plymouth and Cornish Advertiser
West Briton
West Briton and Cornwall Advertiser
Western Morning News

BOOKS

Eddleston, John J., *The Encyclopaedia of Executions* (London; John Blake, 2004)
Hocking, Dr Denis, *Bodies and Crimes* (London; Arrow, 1994)

Certain websites have also been consulted in the compilation of this book, but since they have a habit of disappearing, to avoid frustration, they have not been cited.

INDEX